THE
RIVER

PAUL VASEY

THE RIVER

A MEMOIR OF LIFE
IN THE BORDER CITIES

BIBLIOASIS
Windsor, Ontario

FIRST EDITION

Library and Archives Canada Cataloguing in Publication

Vasey, Paul, author
        The River / Paul Vasey.

Issued in print and electronic formats.
ISBN 978-1-927428-31-3 (pbk.).--ISBN 978-1-927428-32-0 (ebook)

        1. Vasey, Paul. 2. Television personalities--Ontario--Windsor--Biography. 3. Journalists--Ontario--Windsor--Biography. 4. Authors, Canadian (English)--Biography. 5. Canadian Broadcasting Corporation--Biography. 6. Windsor (Ont.)--Biography. I. Title.

PN1992.4.V37A3 2013   791.4502'32092   C2013-906373-0
                                                     C2013-906374-9

Biblioasis acknowledges the ongoing financial support of the Government of Canada through the Canada Council for the Arts, Canadian Heritage, the Canada Book Fund; and the Government of Ontario through the Ontario Arts Council.

Edited by Daniel Wells
Copy-edited by Mary Popovich
Typeset and designed by Kate Hargreaves

PRINTED AND BOUND IN CANADA

For
Liana and Amara
Evan and Eric

Life once lived, the way
you remember it is fiction
—Norman Levine

... and Toad, with no one to check his statements or to criticize in an unfriendly spirit, rather let himself go.

... much that he related belonged more properly to the category of what-might-have-happened-had-I-only-thought-of-it-in-time-instead-of-ten-minutes-afterwards. Those are always the best and raciest adventures; and why should they not be truly ours, as much as the somewhat inadequate things that really come off?
—Kenneth Grahame
The Wind In The Willows

... the lies told by writers are not untruths; they are merely unreal. *Errori non falsi*, Dante, who knew what he was doing, called them, "Lies that are not false." The distinction is important.
—Alberto Manguel
The Unanswerable Question

Tell me about the river, she said.
What do you want to know? he said.
What it means, she said.
Well, he said. Where should I begin?
At the beginning, she said.
Of course, he said.

THIS STORY BEGINS IN THE SUMMER OF 1965——THE SUMMER I turned 20—in a place I thought was called Winzer. Never heard of the place until Art Davidson, my first editor, told me he'd arranged a job for me at *The Winzer Star*.

I'd gone to work for Art at *The Owen Sound Sun-Times* while I was still in high school—youth column, high-school column, summer jobs—and finally pestered him to take me on full-time once I'd managed to escape high school. I worked there for a year and a bit and then—don't ask me why—quit and took a job as a salesman for a local printing company.

Well, actually, there was a reason. My best pal had just landed a job at that firm. His own little office, company car, three times the money I was making at *The Sun-Times*—and like a fool I bit when he said they needed someone else. My gut told me I was being a fool. But like a fool, I ignored my instincts, quit my job at *The Sun-Times*, put on my new brown suit and headed into a whole new world. I knew as I walked into that place on the first day that I'd made a huge mistake—me, a salesman? egad—and quit before I even sat down at the desk they'd cleared out for me.

I couldn't face Art Davidson—it would take a lot of paragraphs to adequately explain how good he'd been to me—and so I waited a week or more before screwing up the courage to climb the stairs to the second-floor newsroom at *The Sun-Times* and ask for my job back.

Art was sitting at the wire desk just inside the newsroom door. He and everyone else in the room did a double take when I turned up at the door in my foolish brown salesman's suit. The look on Art's face said it all. He had just, the day before, hired my replacement. 'I wish you'd let me know sooner,' he said. And there we were on either side of a silence larger than the newsroom. Then he stood up—'Give me a minute'—and crossed the newsroom to his office. Shut the door.

Herby, the wire editor, shook his head. 'He waited a week, hoping you'd call.'

He knew? 'They called him when you quit. Gave him shit for giving them such a good reference for such a little turd.' He shrugged his eyebrows, went back to work. Everyone else was suddenly busy typing or talking on the phone.

I stood there watching Art standing behind his desk talking on the phone. He hung up, crooked his index finger. I crossed the newsroom, opened his office door. 'Shut the door. Sit down.'

Winzer?

Art, still standing behind his desk, scribbled something on a scrap of paper, handed it to me.

'See Norm Hull when you get there. He's the editor. He'll have something for you.'

I started to thank him, to explain what a huge screw-up I was. He waved me off, shaking his head. 'Good luck,' he said.

I opened the door to go, then turned. 'Where's Winzer?'

He smiled, gave his head another shake: 'Get a road map.'

I got the map—oh, *Windsor*—loaded all my earthlies into my chopped-and-channeled '48 Merc coupe (flathead V-8, twin Hollywood mufflers, flat-black paint, spun aluminum hubcaps, your exceedingly evil little hot-rocks auto-*mo*-bile) rumbled up The West

Hill, took one last look as my home town disappeared behind me in the rear-view mirror and went in search of Highway 21, which the map indicated would lead me eventually to Highway 401 and this mysterious southern city where my future, thanks to Art Davidson, was about to unfold.

The Automotive Capital of Canada. Hm.

Pretty amazing city when I got my first glimpse of it, cresting the Jackson Park overpass: A skyline that looked like New York, or what I thought a New York skyline might look like, never having been there either. But appearances can be deceiving. Once I drove all the way down Ouellette Avenue I discovered, as all newcomers do, that the skyline belonged to someone else. There was a river between them and us. Us being Windsor, Ontario, Canada. Them being Detroit, Michigan, U.S. of A.

The Detroit River.

PARK THE CAR. GO DOWN THE INCLINE PAST THE BRITISH AMERICAN HOTEL TO the river's edge. Look upriver and there's Belle Isle with its nifty little bridge connecting to Detroit. Downriver, there's the Ambassador Bridge and beyond it, some kind of nightmare steel mill or something. Look up and down Windsor's riverfront and it's all railway lines and ramps leading to the rail ferries. Not all that pretty. But pretty gritty. All border town.

The River was sure nice to look at, and back then as it is right now it's a magnet. You can't help but stand there and stare, the river rolling past with ducks and gulls on its back, the ocean on its mind.

The Detroit River is about 32 miles long from Windmill Point Light at the head of the river at Lake St. Clair to the Detroit River Light at its mouth in Lake Erie. It flows west from Lake St. Clair but then takes a big graceful turn and flows south past Amherstburg to Lake Erie.

The channel was formed some 10,000 – 12,000 years ago during the retreat of the Wisconsin Glacier. It ranges in width from about a third of a mile to four miles, is 50 feet deep at its deepest point and drops just three feet between Lake St. Clair and Lake Erie. The current is about 1.5 miles per hour and the discharge, approximately 188,000 cubic feet per second, is always constant.

The watershed basin for the Detroit River is approximately 700 square miles. Since it's so short it doesn't have many tributaries: River Rouge and the Ecorse River on the American side, Little River and River Canard on the Canadian.

So it's not much of a river, really. Not like the Mackenzie (4,200 miles) or the Nile (4,000 miles) or the Amazon (4,000 miles) or the Mississippi (3,700 miles) or the Yukon (1,900 miles).

Some people would argue it's not a river at all, but a strait.

Strait? River? River? Strait?

Let's see.

Oxford: River: Copious stream of water flowing in a channel to sea or lake or marsh or another. (*see* rive).

Okay. *Rive:* Rend, cleave ... whence *river.*

Sounds like a river.

But maybe not.

Oxford: Strait: Narrow passage of water connecting two seas or bodies of water.

The French, who happened by on their way to somewhere else in the 1600s, couldn't make up their mind. So they called it *Rivière du Détroit*, which translates literally as "River of the Strait". Which explains the name of our neighbour to the north. Yes. Detroit is north of us, which makes Windsor, Ontario the only city in Canada to be located south of its American neighbour.

Drives tourists crazy: 'Just head north on Ouellette.'

'You mean that way?'

'No, that way.'

'But isn't that Detroit over there?'

'Uh huh.'

Just one of many neat and puzzling things about our town.

For instance, Windsor is on the same latitude as Northern California. Well, almost. Windsor is at 42°18' N latitude and the California-Oregon border is at exactly 42°00' N. Close enough for the tourist bureau, which loves to brag about it.

The touristy types call Windsor The Banana Belt. Only a slight exaggeration: Windsor has the warmest climate of any of Ontario's cities, thanks to the lakes which surround us. We have about two months of winter (January, February). Okay, three (December). There's snow on the ground an average of 50 or so days a year (compared with Winnipeg, where there's snow on the ground for 130). The average temperature in March is 6, in November 8. The rest of the year the temperature is in double digits—and *real* double digits come June, July and August. Hot and muggy.

Where were we?

Yes. The river, or strait, or *river of the strait.* Whatever you call it, the River (rarely do you hear anyone call it by its real name) is so deeply engrained in our consciousness that we refer to it all the time, even when we don't notice that we're talking about it.

For instance: When we're going to Detroit, we go *across the river,* or we go *over the river.* If you're giving someone directions to downtown, 'head down toward the river.' We go *away from the river* when we're heading home to South Windsor. We go *along the river* when we take a drive downriver to Amherstburg and upriver when we head out to Riverside on our way to Belle River (which also has a river, the Belle River, which is a real river and a lovely one, but only half as long as ours).

The River is just part of the fabric of our lives. It's part of our vocabulary. And it's very much a part of who we are and what we do. And we just can't stay away.

We 'go down to the river' and we do so for all sorts of reasons. We go in the winter to see the ice floes, we go in the summer hoping for a little breeze on those 90-degree, 100%-humidity summer scorchers. We go in the daytime and go in the night-time. We go early in the morning to fish or to jog or to walk and we go late at night which, on a windless night, is one of my favourite times to stand by the rail admiring the skyline of Detroit right-side up in the inky sky and upside down on the river's mirrored face. All the better if the spell is broken by a freighter winking past.

We fish in the river, we sail along the river, we marvel at the river in all its moods (I especially love those wild west-wind days when our river, like Margaret Laurence's river in *The Diviners,* decides to flow both ways—the winds pushing whitecaps *up* the river against that formidable current).

And as the old song would have us do:
Yes, we'll gather at the river,
The beautiful, the beautiful river;
Gather with the saints at the river

Well, maybe not the saints. But just about everyone else.
And just about everyone in Windsor has a river story to tell.
All you have to do is ask.

Martin Deck: 'This would have been when I was 14 or 15. We were drinking down by the river. Ten or eleven of us. We always hung out there, across from the Coronation (Tavern, foot of Curry). It was a great spot. The bank was steep and the cops couldn't see us down there. I had an old three-speed bike, banana seat, no gears, no brakes. I used my feet for brakes. I'd had a couple of beers and, what the hell, rode full speed down the hill. Evel Knievel style. I jumped off at the bottom and the bike went right into the river. And that, to me, was the end of it. The bike was gone. But a couple of days later, this friend of mine came by and he had my bike. He'd gone back and jumped in the river and pulled it out. Meant a lot more to him than it did to me.'

Beth MacDonald: 'I remember a huge willow tree down by the river. It's at a house on Riverside Drive between Thomson and Ford. It was a lawyer's house—Bowman, Bill Bowman. He had a daughter, Betsy, who was a year or two younger than me, and we would play out front of their house. They had a boatlift and a breakwall. The willow tree was about halfway down their property toward the water. The trunk of the tree was huge. Three of us with our arms stretched out, that's how wide it was. There was a bench built around it that you could sit on. We used to chase each other around it and the tree was so big you couldn't see the person on the other side.

'Right beside their house was a little tiny house that was knocked down many years ago. At the northeast corner of that property there was a tiny beach and we'd go into the water there. You could swim there and never have a thought about pollution or dirty water or undertow.

'It was all sparkling water then.'

Pat Frezell: 'We lived on Tilston. We used to call the neighbourhood Bridgeview because that's what you saw. The Bridge. There must have been 100 kids in those two blocks. It seemed every family had seven or eight kids. All those good Catholic families.

'I remember walking down to Shore Acres pool. It was a great pool. It's still there, although they've renamed the park. Atkinson Park, I think. We used to walk down there from Tecumseh Road, which was quite a way. I left there when I was twelve, so we were pretty young. But we walked there all the time. I remember going down there with our rolled-up towels. We'd swim for two or three hours. We were famished by the time we headed home.' And this one: 'Do you remember the ship that sank in the river? I forget the name. It was a big ship. My dad came home from work and he said "everyone in the car" and we all got in our big blue family station wagon—all of us, five boys and two girls—and we drove down to the river. And there was the ship. It looked like a great big beached whale. It was amazing.'

Tom Lucier: 'My father told me this one. They used to go swimming from Queen's dock in the west end. At the foot of Mill Street. He remembers there was a dock down by the river where this fat guy lived. Really fat. This guy tied a rope around himself, tied the other end to the dock and jumped in the river and just floated there.' Tom's Dad also told him about the time—'back around 1950 when he was 10 or 12'—when he went down to the river to see "a Negro baptism." Something like 40 people out there, just offshore, in their suits and their dresses. Singing and praying. He was shocked.'

Martin Deck: 'We used to go tobogganing down by the river. Living in Windsor, there weren't many hills. You could go out on the 401 by the overpasses, but that was pretty dangerous. So we went down by the river. Between the bridge and where the CBC is now. It was really steep and great for tobogganing. The trick was to turn the toboggan over and fall off right at the bottom. You had to get off in a hurry. I don't remember anyone ever going right into the river.' Except the night he did. 'When I was about 13, I went jogging with my broth-

er Peter. It was February or March. Freezing, as I recall. We were
jogging along near the foot of Rankin. It was basically a vacant field.
There was an asphalt path by the river, but there was no railing. The
path was about three feet from the river. It was slushy and snowy. It
was only about 7 or 8 at night, but it was pitch dark. I lost my footing
and went right into the river. I thought I was going to die. It wasn't
that deep, but I was convinced the current was going to carry me
away. Peter pulled me out, and I don't remember exactly, but he probably carried me up the embankment and took me to the first house at
the end of Rankin and knocked on the door. The woman let us in and
put me in a hot shower. I remember that.'

Tim Lefaive: 'I used to go down fishing with my brother Reggie. I was
14 or 15. We'd leave home on Dominion (Boulevard) on our bikes—
this would be about four in the morning—and we'd ride down Huron
Line no hands. It was awesome. Try that today. You can hardly cross
the road down there anymore. We'd go down around the salt mines
to fish for pickerel. There was an old structure there with a staircase
zigzagging up the side and we'd climb up there—the staircase was
shaking—to look down on the river and see where the fish were coming up to the surface so we'd know where to go fishing. By 9 or so it
would be getting hot. Reggie's friends used to jump into the river, but
you had to be careful the current wouldn't get you. Some of them tied
a rope around themselves. I never went in. I was too scared. But they
did.' And this one: 'My older brother Richard used to go ice-fishing
down below the bridge. There's a little bay there and there was always
ice collecting in there. He said one time him and another guy were
out there fishing when the ice split. The piece they were on didn't
move, but the piece that broke off was only a couple of feet away. If
they'd have been on that one, they'd have been screwed. It drifted
right out onto the river. Scared the crap out of them.'

And one last one, from Martin Deck: 'Down near the foot of Chewett
was one of the places where folks would go and park their cars. We
were eight or ten. We never knew exactly what they were doing in
those cars. Someone said they were watching submarine races. Some

of the guys, they'd go up and knock on the windows, ask what time it was. I never did that. One night I was there with my brothers. They had me lie on the ground, then they picked me up, hands and feet, and carried me down to the foot of the dock. They made like they were throwing me in—one of my brothers threw a big rock into the water, made a huge splash—but I slipped off the side of the dock and ran off. One of the guys from one of the cars got out and ran down. "What the fuck are you kids doing?" We had a lot of fun down there.'

Kids, eh?

*   *   *

ONE SUNNY SUMMER DAY I WENT DOWN TO THE RIVER AT LUNCHTIME, parked down near the bridge. Right in front of me, sitting on a wooden kitchen chair, there was a fellow pumping a foot-operated wheel of some sort. When I got closer I could see that the vertical wheel was covered with black sandpaper, that really fine kind. And he was busy smoothing the surface of flat rocks, the kind you use for skipping on the water. The ones he'd finished with were in a pile in a cardboard box by his foot.

How can you not ask?

'I paint on them,' he said.

He didn't miss a beat with his right foot, kept pumping the wheel and sanding the stones.

'Paint?'

'Have a look in there,' he said, nodding in the direction of a big fishing tackle box beside the cardboard box. Inside there were six or seven stones on the faces of which he'd painted little river scenes: the pilot boat moored beyond the bridge on the far side of the river; the Boblo ferry *Columbia*; the bridge; a passing freighter. They were finely detailed and very accomplished. Made you wonder why he didn't do his painting on paper or canvas. Which seemed like a good question to ask him.

'I love the feel of the stones,' he said. 'And they seem to suggest the sort of painting they'd like to wear.'

Which seemed to be a pretty fair answer.

'You come down here very often?'

'Every day,' he said, 'since I got out.'

'Out?'

'I did life,' he said.

'Life?'

'Yeah.'

I waited.

'What for?'

'Stupidity,' he said.

He finished the stone he was sanding, placed it in the cardboard box, selected another and started sanding.

I waited. He sanded.

'Stupidity?' I said.

'Quit school when I was 16. Life on the assembly line is what you get when you're that stupid.' He smiled. 'If you spend your life in a factory, this is just about exactly where you want to spend all your time once you get out.'

'I guess you would.' I thanked him for chatting with me. Told him I hoped he'd have a good day.

'All my days are good days now,' he said.

Running into people like him is a huge part of the charm of heading down to the River. We love just to sit and watch the river and all the other people who have come to watch the river. Which is precisely what I'm doing this Wednesday afternoon in mid-March. It's one of those beautiful summer-like days we sometimes get in early spring: 74 degrees with a brilliant sun and those tufty, snowy-white clouds which zeppelin along over the skyline of Detroit.

I'm in Ambassador Park, the park by the bridge, which also happens to be roughly the spot where a band of Jesuits stepped ashore in 1728, took a look around and thought this would be an ideal spot to start their mission to the Huron Indians. According to the book *Essex County Sketches,* 'A Jesuit priest arrived in Detroit and soon established a mission on the opposite shore where the village of Sandwich grew up many years later. The mission house, part of which remained until the early years of the present century, was built partly of hewed pine and partly of sawn lumber and measured thirty by forty-five feet. In later years, a church was erected and also a priest's residence, a storehouse for furs and one for provisions, and a blacksmith shop.'

The Jesuits eventually moved downriver to Bois Blanc Island (Bob-lo these days), then moved again to what is now the American side. The proselytizing did not go all that well. The Hurons burned the mission to the ground in 1747.

Settlers had better luck. The first French families arrived at this same spot around 1748 and thought it would be a dandy place to start farming, which they did. Quite successfully.

Many land grants were made in the 30 years leading up to 1760, many to ex-soldiers. Long thin Quebec-style farms, each with river frontage, each extending hundreds of acres inland. Lots of advantages: Lots of wood, wild berries and wild game at the back of the farm, a road up by the river by which they could get their grain to the local windmill for grinding, and easy access to the water if they wanted to get somewhere by boat.

By the 1820s, more newcomers: Slaves who fled their masters in Kentucky arrived in the area almost weekly and began to do, as free men, what they had learned to do as slaves: Raise tobacco. Hundreds of them settled in Sandwich and Amherstburg.

Windsor became a village in 1854, a town four years later and a full-fledged city in 1892. Which makes Windsor the oldest continually settled area west of Quebec in Canada. Something else the tourist types love to tout.

THERE'S A LINE-UP AT TERRY'S HOME-MADE FRIES TRUCK AT THE EDGE OF THE parking lot just below Riverside Drive and the lot is full. In fact it's so full at 1:30 in the afternoon that some people are risking tickets in the no-parking zones because there's no where else to park, and how can you pass up a day beside the river on a day like this?

A gentleman in short-sleeves and sunglasses has parked himself in a lawn chair in the shade of a tree which is already budding out. I settle in at a picnic table a few feet away.

'Perfect day to be down by the river.'

'Yes sir. It certainly is.'

There's general agreement on that front. Dozens of people (shouldn't they be at work, or school or somewhere?) have decided to join us.

Three university-age young women have spread a red blanket on the slope behind Terry's truck and seem to be enjoying the fries. A girl in jean shorts, white T-shirt and sunglasses walks by, ponytail swinging as she goes. A pair of Canadian geese honk hello as they head for a splashdown on the river. A man zips along in his wheelchair, Canada flag flapping from the antennae attached to the back of his seat. A young mother pushes a stroller and chats with her girlfriend as dad brings up the rear, baby in sunhat asleep on his shoulder. A 20-something roller-blader passes them, heading toward the bridge, headset clamped over his ball cap.

Out on the river, some fishermen are heading upstream looking for a better spot and, a little further out from shore, two guys and a girl head the other way on a pontoon boat. Another outboard zips upriver and a train sounds its whistle on the far shore. Trucks are lined up halfway across the Ambassador Bridge. Nice view while the truckers are waiting to make their way into the U.S.

Two gulls which were having an argument over some of Terry's fries take to the air as a shirtless kid in a top-down Jeep rolls into the parking lot—no stereo on a day like this?—looking for a spot. He looks around at all the cars parked where they should and shouldn't be and gives up.

Patience—as James Joyce pointed out—'is the great thing.' If Jeep boy had waited another two minutes, he'd have been in luck. Instead, the long-haired dude on his Harley who has just rolled down from the Drive discovers it's his lucky day: A mom and dad are just packing their stroller and their baby into their minivan, ready to head for home. Motorcycle dude lights a smoke and sits and waits.

Who else? Dozens and dozens of people. Have a look: A teenaged boy in shorts and long-sleeved white shirt riding his bicycle, headset over his backwards baseball cap; a woman in her 20s—a character right out of Chekhov—walking her little white dog on a leash; a woman jogging in grey shorts, purple top, white ball cap and pink running shoes; a lad, maybe ten or eleven, on his bike, fishing gear—tackle box, bait pail, rod and net—in the handle-bar carrier; a 50-ish fellow, rod in one hand, white plastic bait pail in the other; a skinny white-haired gent wearing a broad-brimmed birder hat, knee-length shorts, blue socks and running shoes. I could go on and on. But you get the picture.

Wasn't always this way. There was a time, not all that long ago, when our riverfront looked like the riverfront directly across the way: One giant railyard, the riverbank a mess of weeds and scraps of paper, pop cans and broken bottles and out-of-control shrubs. Not very inviting, and not a spot you would go for a stroll. Certainly not at night. Unless you were looking for trouble. Who knew what was lurking down there? Actually, the cops knew what was lurking down there. And tub-thumping preachers. And editorial writers. Trouble. Capital T. Back then the riverfront was a favourite haunt of winos (keeping dry drinking and sleeping in the railway underpasses) and hookers (male and female) and shady characters hoping to make a quick score on an unsuspecting someone wandering down looking for a little action. Let's just say that when I first came to Windsor back in the 1960s the riverfront was not a place you would take out-of-town guests to impress them. And it wasn't in the tourist brochures.

So this is Winzer. With a D and an S not a Z and an E, though if you asked anyone then or anyone today the name of the city where they live they would pronounce it just as Art Davidson had: *Winzer*.

*   *   *

NORM HULL LOOKED MORE OR LESS AS YOU'D EXPECT THE EDITOR OF A BIG metropolitan daily to look: White hair, what was left of it, white shirt and blue tie, grey trousers which were an inch or two too short (all his trousers, as it would turn out, were an inch or two too short). He sounded just like Art Davidson and perhaps all other newspaper editors of the time: As though he'd just missed a deadline and it was your fault. He led me across the newsroom and into his office. Nice view of the river and the office buildings of Detroit on the far side. He sat down in a very large leather chair behind a very large wooden desk, indicating I should take one of the straight-backed wooden chairs facing it. 'You'll start tomorrow,' he said.

I should mention that I'd spent the drive down from Owen Sound, and the previous evening sitting in the very elegant bar of The Norton Palmer Hotel, rehearsing what I would say in my job interview with *The Editor* of an award-winning *big-city* newspaper. Quite a little speech as I recall, which I never got to give and Norm never got to hear.

Three words from him and that was the end of the interview.

'Where are you staying?'

'The Norton Palmer.'

'You can't stay there on the wages I'll be paying you.' He took the cap off his fountain pen and scratched something on a scrap of paper, held it across the desk. 'Go to this address. It's a rooming house. On twenty bucks a week it's something you can afford. And it'll do until you can find something better.'

We sat there looking at each other for a few seconds.

'That's it?' I said.

'Don't be late,' he said.

'Thank you,' I said, and stood up.

He was already busy reading some proofs on his desk.

*   *   *

THE ROOMING HOUSE WAS A THREE-STOREY CLAPBOARD AFFAIR——PAINTED A God-awful pea-green—squatting on a corner lot a few blocks south of downtown. There was a verandah across the front. I parked on the side street, cut across the lawn and climbed the steps to the very impressive front door—from the days when the place was a home, not a rooming house—with a bell you rang by twisting a little brass handle in the centre of the door just below the bevelled glass window. 'Come in. Ain't locked.'

Open the door, there was a central hall leading to a staircase. There were double doors leading to rooms on either side of the hall. The ones on the left were closed, the little window panes covered on the inner side by sheer drapes through which you could just make out the shadow of things—chairs and a bureau and a bed. The doors on the right were open.

The first thing you noticed about the Landlady was her size. She was huge. I mean, really huge. Fat-lady-in-the-circus huge. She had wedged herself into an extra-wide armchair in her room. You had to wonder how she'd ever get herself back up on her feet. That huge. The other thing you noticed right away—after the shock of her size—was her eyes. Brilliant blue and, magnified by her Coke-bottle glasses, about twice of the size of normal eyes. All the better to see you with.

Her armchair was in the centre of what would have been a living room when the place was a home, not a rooming house. There was a big stone fireplace in the centre of the wall behind her, little stained glass windows high up on either side. Would have been a classy room—fancy scrolling on the cove ceiling, oak window frames and door frames—back when a bank manager or a businessman had called it home. But she had turned it into a kind of one-room apartment—bed by the front window, table and chairs by the back wall, armchair dead centre so she could see everyone coming and going in the hallway. During the months I stayed there her doors were never shut, day or night. She was a watcher.

'Mister Hull said you'd be calling.'

Like it was some kind of social visit.

She asked me about myself. I told her my name, where I was from.

She said she had one room available. 'Number Five.' It was on the third floor. 'There's a fire escape,' she said. This was not as reassuring as she had apparently meant it to be.

'Most of my boys have been with me quite some time. I have very little turnover, but if someone does leave you'll be next in line for a larger room. Go up and see it. If it suits you it's twenty dollars a month.'

I told her I was sure it would be fine.

'See it first. You should never take anything sight unseen.' The first of the Landlady's many words of wisdom.

'You'll see the Rules of the House on the way up.'

She'd printed the rules in big block letters on pieces of scrap paper which she'd taped to the faded flowered wallpaper all the way up the stairs, which made you wonder how she'd managed to make it all the way up and back down again, considering it seemed to be all she could do to sit and draw breath at the same time.

NO ALCOHOL
NO FEMALE VISITORS AT ANY TIME!
NO NOISE AFTER NINE P.M.
TURN OUT THE LIGHTS
And so on.

Room Five was straight-ahead, top of the stairs. It was maybe twelve feet by twelve. Bed, bedside table with a lamp, a three-drawer bureau, an armchair by the window which afforded an excellent view of the alley which ran behind the house. Smelled of mothballs. Could have been worse. But not much. It would do until I could find something bigger. And better. As Mister Hull would say: 'It'll keep the rain off your head for the time being. Once you've met some of the other fellows, maybe two or three of you can go in on an apartment.'

The washroom—one for all five roomers—was back on the second floor. Tile floor, yellow-painted (but not recently) walls, clawfoot tub with plastic flowered shower curtain.

On the wall beside the tub:

SHOWERS FIVE MINUTES

On the wall above the toilet:

IF YOU'RE READING THIS THE SEAT SHOULD BE UP!!

On the wall beside the sink:

CLEAN UP AFTER YOURSELF

On the wall beside the door:

SHUT THE LIGHTS

It wasn't clear whether she meant we should shower in the dark.

The Landlady was exactly where I'd left her, sheathed in a pale pink and purple house dress, bunny slippers complete with floppy ears. 'So?'

'It's fine. I'll take it.'

'First and last month in advance. Cash only, no cheques. Rent is due every first of the month.'

I paid.

'A receipt?'

'You don't need a receipt. You got my word.'

She gave me one of those grandmotherly smiles.

'A key?'

'You don't need a key, honey. This is the kind of place you break out of, not into.'

Another smile.

'Thanks,' I said. 'I'll go get my stuff.'

I went out onto the porch. The passenger-side door was open. There was a kid standing beside the car. His buddy was in the passenger seat, rifling through my duffel bag.

'Hey!'

The kid on the sidewalk, he just stood there looking at me. I ran down the stairs and across the lawn and I couldn't believe the little shit was still standing there. Smirking. I went to grab him and he kneed me where it hurts the most and I went down like a bag of hammers. I could hear the kid in the car laughing, then saying 'grab this,' and as I was trying to get to my knees and then my feet the kid who'd kneed me kicked me in the ribs—hard—and I went down again. Man, the pain. By the time I got up, the kids, and my duffel bag, were long gone. Lucky for me that the rest of my clothes and the rest of my stuff were locked in the trunk.

'You're sure of a welcome in Windsor, coz…'

*   *   *

You're making this up.
No, he said.
This rooming house really existed?
Did indeed.
And the Landlady?
Larger than life, he said.
All those signs on the walls?
Too many to count, he said.
Hm.
And the kids? she said.
I can still feel the pain.

*   *   *

THE BANDIT'S CAFÉ WAS ACROSS FROM *THE STAR*, A LITTLE CORNER PLACE, Pitt and Ferry.

Benny Grant, pint-sized genius editor, hung the handle on him: 'No matter what he charges you,'—bacon, eggs and toast was thirty cents —'it's robbery. He's a friggin' bandit.' Benny was right about that. Drop into The Bandit's and you were guaranteed lots of coffee—all you could drink for a dime—lots of grease with your eggs. And lots of attitude.

The restaurant door was at the corner. There were windows along the Ferry Street side. Open the door, the place smelled of bacon and coffee and cigarette smoke.

The counter was on the right as you walked in. Just inside the door, beside the cash register, there was a pile of newspapers, greasy fingerprint smudges on them all. If you were lucky you might find today's paper. Otherwise it was a history lesson. No matter what time you walked through the door there were people hunched on the stools along the counter, hands cradling a mug, reading *The Star*. The booths were along the Ferry Street windows. Winter-to-spring they were always fogged up, all the hot air inside. You could sit in one of the booths and do a little drawing with your finger.

The Bandit was a short guy, slicked-back black hair with a pronounced widow's peak—a sort of pudgy pint-sized Jack Nicholson— big gut behind an apron that looked like it might last have been washed a couple of years earlier. They say you should never trust a skinny cook. Sometimes you shouldn't trust the fat ones either.

'Hey Bandit.'

This was one of the Trench Coats at the counter.

'Hey yourself.'

The Bandit didn't look up. He was busy with a couple of orders of eggs. There was a mound of bacon sizzling at the edge of the grill. It was one of those big industrial stoves with a flat black top. The Bandit cracked the eggs and dropped them on the blacktop and let them bubble away until the edges had turned all curly and brown, then he'd run the flipper under them and slide them on a plate, flipper some bacon beside them, wait for the toast to pop, slather some butter on it. 'Order's up.' Which meant you could go up to the counter and get the plate yourself. Sort of semi-self-serve.

The Bandit gave me the eye when I walked in. A cigarette was wedged in the corner of his mouth. With any luck, the ash would drop before he turned back to the stove. 'What'll it be?'

'Double shot of whisky. Light on the ice.'

'Very funny, Hemingway.'

'All right. How about bacon and eggs. Side of toast. Dry. No butter.'

I grabbed one of the booths, right at the end where you could get a faint whiff of the bathrooms in the back. Lit a smoke, spread out my paper. 'What's the chance of a coffee?'

'What's the chance you'll grab a mug and help yourself?' Which meant that Mrs. Bandit was either busy in the back or taking the day off.

'You been here three times already. That makes you a regular.'

I helped myself to a coffee, feeling like a part of things. 'Is it cheaper when I pour it myself?'

'Yeah,' said the Bandit. 'You don't have to leave yourself a tip.' He smiled. There went the ash. He scraped it off the stove with his flipper. 'Plus it's hotter than if you wait for me to get it.'

'Ha ha.'

'Ha ha yourself.'

I took my mug back to my booth. Ten minutes later the Bandit slid my plate onto the counter. 'Order's up.' Two eggs over easy in a little puddle of grease, a clump of bacon, two slices of toast soaked with butter.

'Dry toast,' I said.

'What?'

'Dry toast. I like my toast dry.'

'Why didn't you say so?'

'I said so.'

'You never said nothin' about no butter.' He grabbed the toast off the plate and tossed it into the trash. If I was lucky he'd remember to push the lever down on the toaster in the next five or ten minutes. Didn't look like he was in any mood to mess with. He slid another plate onto the counter. 'Order's up.'

The Beatles were on the radio. Paperback Writer. 'You hear what John Lennon said?' This was the Trench Coat at the counter. You could tell what was coming next. 'Bigger than Jesus? Where's he get off?'

'He's probly right.' This was the Old Doll beside him. 'Kids nowadays. Who goes to church? Who believes in anything anymore?'

'They believe in free love,' said the Trench Coat.

'They'll rue the day,' said the Old Doll. 'Mark my words. They'll rue the day.'

I folded my newspaper in half, propped it against the sugar container.

Black kids were rioting in L.A. Protests against the war in Vietnam were getting bigger and noisier.

'Toast's up, Hemingway.'

'Thanks.'

Self-serve. I slid back into my booth, turned to the sports pages.

What about that Denny McLain? Not even August and 13 wins. How good is this guy anyway?

Things had quieted down. The Bandit looked around. 'Anyone wants a refill, you know where the pot is. I'm takin' a break.'

He poured himself a coffee, came around from behind the counter, wedged himself into the other side of my booth. 'You a fight fan?'

'Won my weight class once,' I said.

'When was that?'

'When I was ten.'

He smiled.

'That was it for my career in the ring,' I said.

'I've got a story for you.'

'Shoot,' I said.

'There's a guy in town who once fought Joe Louis.'

'You're kidding, right?'

He shook his head. 'Name's Al Borshuk. Fought under the name of Al Delaney. Great story, if you get him talking.'

'Thanks,' I said.

'First, you'll have to find him.'

'Any clues?'

'Any bar downtown.'

'Thanks,' I said.

'You're welcome,' he said. 'This is one story of yours that might be worth readin'.' Big smile.

*   *   *

SULTRY NIGHTS. YOU KNOW HOW SOMETIMES LIFE TAKES YOU BY SURPRISE? This girl, we'd gotten together a few times and we'd hit it off pretty well, anyway, she and her mother lived in a sprawling ranch-style house down on the Drive, backing onto the river across from Belle Isle. Sweet place. Sweet girl. This time I'm talking about, the girl's mother was off travelling somewhere or other—they were one of those world-travelling families—so the girl had one of her friends come down to stay with her. Made the place a little less spooky come night-time. But it got spooky anyway. They were just hanging out—watching TV or listening to the stereo—when they heard this weird little noise. Scritch scratch. Like that. Next morning they go out to have a look around, and sure enough there were all these scratch marks on the side door, someone trying to break in. So now they're really spooked. This girl, the one whose mother owned the place, she says I'm going to ask this friend of mine to come down and stay with us.

Guess who's the lucky friend?

So I hung up the phone and packed my (replacement) duffel bag, slid into my Merc coupe and a few minutes later there we were, the three of us: My friend, her very delightful dark-haired brown-eyed girlfriend and me sipping whisky (me) and rye and Cokes (them) down by the river, watching the freighters throb past on their way to who knew where. Very congenial. Which is Part One of the Life Surprise I mentioned.

Part Two. I'd been bunking over a couple of nights when my friend, she gets a call from someone out west—Manitoba, Saskatchewan, wherever—telling her that one of her relatives had died and that the funeral was going to be the day after tomorrow and they—all the western relatives—were hoping she and her Mom could fly out. My friend explained about her Mom being in Africa or South America or wherever it was her mother had flown off to and that there was no way she could track her down but, yes, she would fly out. So we, her dark-haired brown-eyed friend and I, drove her out to the airport first thing next morning and watched and waved as the plane lifted into the clear-blue cloudless summer morning, and there we were, two strangers who'd somehow stumbled into each other's lives in what can only be described, you'll have to agree, as a very weird way.

Then?

Well, we get into my very sweet '48 Merc coupe with the fuzzy dice hanging from the rear-view and the extremely cool, I thought, 8-ball gear-shift knob, and we rolled out of the parking lot, the flat-head V-8 thrumming in a provocative way through those twin Hollywood mufflers, and my new pal, she's looking straight-ahead and not saying a word until she looks down at the pavement through the hole in the passenger-side floorboards (what were left of them).

'Different,' she says.

And there's that smile, which could cause a fellow to drive right off the road and into the ditch. Twenty minutes later, we're back at our friend's big river-facing art-filled house and we pour a couple of coffees and head down to the Muskoka chairs and look at Belle Isle and spend a few minutes contemplating this very peculiar set of circumstances in which we find ourselves.

'So,' I said.

'So,' she said. 'I called my brothers.'

'Brothers?'

'They're going to come down and keep us company.' A Mona Lisa-like smile.

Not precisely what I'd had in mind.

However, the brothers didn't much get in the way. The four of us had a pretty good time—particularly her 14-year-old brother, who thought he'd died and gone to heaven—drinking and playing Scrabble. And they were savvy enough (and the youngster drunk enough) to end up spending most of their time on the couch watching TV (older brother) or sleeping (younger brother) while the two of us spent our late evening and some late nights down by the river talking. Talking about what, exactly, I don't recall. Kierkegaard, most likely. I was in a big buzz about Kierkegaard that summer—his great leap of faith, which seems kind of funny now since I was apparently not too good at leaping and would count myself among those of little faith.

Anyway, the week went by in a flash. My dark-haired brown-eyed girl did not, after all, have to scream for her brothers to come running to the rescue, and the next thing you know she and I are back at the airport and our friend comes through the gate and we're both standing there beaming at her and the first words out of her mouth—I'm quoting directly here—were: 'Well. I see things have changed.'

Yes indeed. Very perceptive.

The dark-haired brown-eyed girl and I would be engaged a couple of months later and married the following summer.

The news rippled out, the way news does.

'You two should elope.' This was the grandmother of my friend, the one with the big house on the river. Florence ('You can call me Flo') had achieved that age—seventy-something I'd say—which gives one the right to say whatever is on her mind. In this case: 'Weddings are just such a pain. All the planning, all the troublesome relatives. All the expense. It's just *too* exhausting.' I told her we'd think it over. 'Believe me, dear, eloping is absolutely your best bet.' Good advice. But like lots of good advice, I let it slide. Flo lit another cigarette— these were the days when everyone smoked—and dropped another couple of ice cubes in her gin and looked for a few moments at the river, then turned to look at me. 'Where are you living?'

I told her.

'A rooming house?'

'Yes,' I said. I provided a few of the details: A brief description of the house and a somewhat longer description of the Landlady. I mentioned The Rules of the House taped to pretty well every wall in the place.

'Sounds dreadful,' she said. She didn't know the half of it. I didn't mention the strange moaning noises I heard in the middle of the night from the room next to mine, a room occupied by a wizened little gnome with a beard and ponytail, nor did I mention the gangly spaced-out stranger down on the second floor who regularly disobeyed the Five Minute Shower Rule and seemed disinclined to observe the Lift The Seat Rule.

'How on earth did you ever end up in such a place?'

'Mister Hull had recommended it,' I said. 'As a temporary way station.'

She drew on her Viceroy, exhaled, looking a little like Bette Davis. 'Norman should know better than to put his boys in a place like that.

You're writing stories. You don't want to become a story.' She smiled. Sipped her gin. Found it to her liking. 'I have something much more suitable in mind.'

Serendipity.

'Something more suitable' turned out to be another big place—red brick, cedar-shake roof, stained-glass windows—down along the river, a few blocks east of my friend's mother's place. 'Ethel Walters is a dear friend of mine. She's too old to be living all alone in that huge old house, which she won't admit, and needs someone to take care of the place when she's away on her little jaunts, which she will admit. You'll be just perfect. You'll love her.'

She asked about my arrangement at the Landlady's.

'Month to month.'

'Well, this is the end of the month. Give your notice tonight. You can move into Ethel's place on the weekend.'

I said it sounded interesting. 'But shouldn't we let Mrs. Walters decide?'

'Of course,' she said. She placed her glass on a coaster and picked up the telephone. 'Ethel. It's Flo. I've found just the young man for you.' Two or three minutes later she hung up, picked up her glass and raised it in my direction. 'All settled.'

And so it was.

And so that Friday after work I parked the Merc in the driveway beside Mrs. Walter's '56 Cadillac convertible—white with a red-leather interior—and rang the doorbell.

Ethel opened the door. 'Well,' she said, giving me the once over. Sly smile in those sapphire eyes. Extended a hand, which I shook. 'Come in. Come in.'

Bird-like would describe her. Bird-like and bejeweled. She had an enormous diamond engagement ring on her left hand, and an impressive diamond-circled ruby on her right. Had to be ten or twenty thousand dollars worth of diamonds in her necklace. And another five or so in her earlobes. Looked like she kept Birks in business.

She was in her seventies—upper-seventies, I guessed. Tiny. Five foot and not much more, but seemed even shorter because of her stooped shoulders. Elegant: Silver hair carefully done and framing a narrow and surprisingly youthful face. She had a weakness for expensive silk dresses and high-heeled shoes. She looked like she might have been on her way to a cocktail party.

She had, as I would discover, a weakness for duMaurier cigarettes all day long and Canadian Club whisky any time after noon.

I was about to kick off my shoes. 'No, no, dear. Leave them on. Let's have a little look around, shall we?'

'Sure, that would be fine.'

'How about a drink first?'

'Sure, that would be fine,' I said.

She led me into the kitchen. 'Whisky?'

'Yes, thanks.'

'Help yourself.' She pointed to a silver tray on the sideboard, crystal whisky glasses circling a decanter whose facets glistened in the sun slanting in through the river-facing windows. 'The ice is in here.' She lifted the lid of a silver ice bucket beside the tray, pincered a couple of cubes into her own glass, held it out to be refilled, then dropped a couple of cubes into my glass.

I poured a little whisky from the decanter into her glass, and then a little into my own.

'That won't last long,' she said, looking at my glass, then her own. I topped hers up, then mine.

'Cigarette?' She offered me one of hers. I lit hers, then mine.

'Now, let's have a little tour shall we?' She led me out of the kitchen into the room next door—floor-to-ceiling double doors and huge windows overlooking the lawn, which sloped down to the river. There were gardens bordering the lot on either side and, by the river, a patio with tables and chairs. 'My favourite place,' she said. 'There's nothing quite like it, having a cocktail by the river, watching the boats go by.' And, as though on command, a freighter loomed into view. 'This, obviously, is the dining room.' The side and back walls were wainscotted in what looked like oak. There was a huge table, four chairs on either side, big armchairs at the head and foot. 'I keep the liquor in here,' she said, tapping the door of an ornate hutch with the pointed toe of one of her high-heeled shoes. 'Help yourself. Every now and then when you think you've had about a bottle you can buy another. Same goes for the fridge. Have anything you like and replace what you eat.'

The living room was behind the dining room. Twice the size, extending three quarters the length of the house on the side facing the road. In the centre of the outer wall there was a marble-faced fireplace above which were a pair of little paintings—maybe eight-by-ten inches—illuminated by tiny lights hovering above each of them.

'Beautiful,' I said.

'They were a gift,' she said. 'Of the artists.'

'That one,' she said, indicating the one on the left, 'is by Tom Thomson. The other is by A.Y. Jackson. They were painted the same day—the summer of 1914—in Algonquin Park. Tom was on a little canvas-seated folding stool facing one way. Alex was seated on a stool behind him, facing the other way. They often did that, took sketching trips together. That's where we met them.

'In fact, we met them the day they'd done these sketches. We were on our honeymoon, staying at a camp owned by a friend of theirs. We all had dinner together. A wonderful time. Anyway, my husband ended up playing cards with them. Drinks and cards. They got on famously. He asked them about their work. They talked for hours. Next morning, when we were getting ready to leave, they gave us these sketches they'd done the day before. As a wedding gift.'

She reached up and removed the Thomson from its mooring, turned it over and showed it to me. 'To my new friends Ethel and William.' It was signed, simply, Tom. She replaced the painting. 'Alex signed his as well.'

She laughed. 'We really had no idea who they were—we thought they were just a couple of young painters—until we got home. Bill had a friend who owned an art gallery. He asked him if he'd ever heard of these young artists we'd just met.' She laughed again.

'Let's go upstairs, shall we? I'll show you to your room.'

My 'room' was over the garage. It was twice as large as most hotel rooms I'd ever seen. Must've been thirty feet by twenty. Pine-paneled, broadloomed floor. Just inside the door, on the left, there was a desk and chair; to the right a love seat and coffee table; against the far wall a double bed. There were bookshelves along all the walls.

'Feel free to browse,' she said.

'The bathroom is through there,' she said, indicating a door beside the desk. Sink, toilet, tub and separate shower. No notices taped to the walls.

'What do you pay presently?'

'Twenty a month,' I said.

'Would that do?'

Do?

'That'll do just fine,' I said.

She extended her hand. 'Deal,' she said. 'How's your drink?'

Both our drinks needed refreshing. We headed back down to the kitchen. I did the refreshing, she added the ice. We sat at the counter facing out over the back lawn.

'There's something I should mention,' she said.

I looked at her. She smiled.

'I travel,' she said. 'Quite a lot.'

'I heard,' I said.

'So I hope you won't mind being alone in the house.'

'Won't bother me,' I said.

'For months,' she said. 'It's one of the reasons I was interested in having someone live here. So the place won't be empty. Please be forthright.'

Forthright? How terrible would this be? Living in a sprawling old house on the river all by myself? I smiled. 'Honestly,' I said. 'I wouldn't mind a bit.'

'You may have friends over, of course.'

Of course.

'As a matter of fact, I have a trip coming up next month.'

'Where are you going?'

'Africa,' she said. 'I'm going on a safari.'

I couldn't help myself. I laughed. 'A safari? Elephants and camels?'

'No.' She laughed as well. 'No camels or elephants. Or tents. We'll be in an air-conditioned motor coach. We'll be touring from one hotel to another playing bridge.'

'Bridge? You're going to Africa to play bridge?'

'It's called a bridge circus. And actually that's quite appropriate. The last one turned out to be exactly that. There were a few quite unfortunate players and the bridge master wasn't quite what he'd held himself out to be. This one should be better. Mister Sharif is organizing it.'

'Mister Sharif?'

'Omar. The actor. Perhaps you've heard of him?'

'Yes,' I said. 'I have.'

'He's charming,' she said. 'And a deadly player.'

'How long is your trip?'

'Two months.'

'You'll be playing bridge for two months?'

'Only in the evenings. During the day I expect we'll be looking at elephants and giraffes and lions.'

'Sounds like fun,' I said.

'Oh,' she said. 'It'll be grand fun.' She lifted her glass, empty except for the remainders of a couple of ice cubes. 'Another?'

'Sure.' I did the honours again.

'There's something I'd like to ask you,' she said.

'Ask away,' I said.

'I wonder if, while I'm away, you wouldn't mind driving my car from time to time. I don't like my cars to sit idle too long. I don't think it's good for them.'

'Sure,' I said.

'I'll have you put on my policy,' she said. 'Just in case.'

'And another thing,' she said. 'I wonder, if I opened an account in your name, whether you'd be good enough to attend to my bills while I'm away. I think three thousand should do it.'

Three thousand dollars? More than what I'd make in three years.

'Yes,' I said. 'That should certainly do it.'

'Wonderful,' she said, and raised her glass. 'And, of course, since you'll technically be working for me, taking care of the house, paying the bills, keeping cobwebs off the car and so forth, I shan't charge you rent while I'm gone.'

'That's not necessary,' I said.

'It's entirely necessary,' she said. 'And as my late husband learned quite early on, I do not like to be argued with.'

She smiled.

You had to like a smile like that.

*　　　*　　　*

Oh, come on. You don't expect me to believe this. Tom Thomson?
Yup.
A.Y. Jackson and Omar Sharif?
All true.
Go on, she said. Can't be true.
Every word, he said. And it gets better.
Better?
Just wait.

*　　　*　　　*

I WAS WORKING LATE. HAD A CUP OF MACHINE COFFEE BESIDE THE TYPEWRITER. It was cold. And there was a disgusting looking scummy film on the surface.

'Jeez.'

I looked up. Larry the Janitor was staring down at my coffee.

'You don't mind me sayin' so, Hemingway. But that coffee looks colder than a corpse and at least as disgustin'.' He gave me one of his patented smiles, reached down into his canvas dustbin on wheels and fished out a mickey. 'Here,' he said. 'This'll put some lead in your pencil.' He topped up my coffee.

'Thanks.'

'Don't mention it.'

He took a sip from the bottle, screwed on the top and dropped it into his trash bin.

'What else you got down there?'

'Oh, you'd be surprised.' He laughed.

'Anything to eat?'

'Half a muffin someone left in the lunchroom.'

'I think I'll stick with your whisky.'

'You can never go wrong with whisky.' He was looking at the paper I had in the typewriter. 'Whatcha workin' on?'

'Homework.'

'Homework?'

'Just checking up on a fighter named Al Delaney. Ever hear of him?'

'Who hasn't? Famous guy. Fought Joe Louis once.'

'So I hear.'

'Check him out. There must be stuff in the morgue about him.'

'Yeah,' I said. 'I'll do that.' I held up the file folder with Al's name typed on the tab.

'Way ahead of me, Hemingway. As usual.' He gave me a pat on the shoulder and headed off, pushing his cart ahead of him. 'I'll be back to check on your coffee in a while.'

Al Borshuk was born in Oshawa, June 14, 1916, moved to Windsor when he was a kid. Started boxing when he was fifteen. One of his first instructors was Patsy Drouillard, the legendary Windsor boxer, who retired as Canadian Lightweight Champion in 1917. Al turned professional in 1934, changed his professional name to Al Delaney and right out of the chute won his first nine bouts in Detroit.

And there it was, in black and white.

'On November 11, 1934, Al Delaney, only 18 years of age, fought Joe Louis at the Detroit Naval Armoury before a packed house. Although Louis won the fight, he sustained the hardest blow he had ever absorbed in a boxing ring, a right hand which broke a molar. 'They never knew how close I came to losing,' said the famed Brown Bomber.' Joe Louis was only 20 at the time. Still.

Al's most notable accomplishment, apart from once being in the ring with Joe Louis, was winning the Canadian heavyweight championship, which he did in Glace Bay, Nova Scotia on May 24, 1941, when he went 12 rounds with Terence "Tiger" Warrington and won by unanimous decision. You can look it all up on the website of the Windsor Essex County Hall of Fame:

> Delaney fought five men who held World Titles. He fought to a draw with a former Light Heavyweight champion George Nichols in 1932. In 1935 he fought to a draw with a former World Light Heavyweight champion Tommy Loughran (1927-29).
>
> In 1936 he easily defeated Two Ton Tony Galento, who fought Joe Louis for the Heavyweight title in 1939. In 1940 he defeated future World Light-Heavyweight champion Gus Lesnevich (1941-48) in an 8-rounder in Brooklyn. In 1944 he lost to Freddie Mills, World Light-Heavyweight champion from 1948-50.

Delaney also had fights with Buddy Baer and Bob Pastor, both of whom fought Joe Louis for the Heavyweight crown. He retired from boxing in 1944.

His career record was 48 wins, 29 losses.

There was a man I wanted to meet.

*   *   *

SOMEONE TOLD ME I MIGHT FIND AL DELANEY DOWN AT THE KILLARNEY. The Killarney had a check-your-weapons reputation. It had earned it. The bartender was a chubby guy, perched on a stool in a corner behind the bar. He was watching TV. He took his time acknowledging my presence. He waited until there was a commercial. Then he tongued his cigar butt from one side of his mouth to the other. 'What'll it be?'

I told him who I was looking for.

'Who's doin' the lookin'?'

I told him who I was, that I wanted to do a story about Al Delaney.

'You want him to string two words together you better get him in the mornin'.'

His was not the kind of grin you'd want to see on a man to whom you owed the rent money.

'You know where I can find him?'

'Coulda found him here fifteen minutes ago.'

The bartender came out from behind the bar and crossed the room, heading for the door.

We were out on the sidewalk. The bartender looked east, then west. 'Couldn't have gone all that far. Shape he's in. Try The Highway. Goes there sometimes.'

'What's he look like?'

'Big guy. Six-two. Six-three. Silver hair, slicked right back.' He pushed his nose to one side with his thumb. 'You'll know you're lookin' at a fighter.' He smiled. Same smile.

I gave him my card. I told him if Al came in 'buy him a beer and keep him here and give me a call.' He said 'sure' but you could tell there'd be two moons in the sky before he'd do any such thing.

Didn't matter. Open the door at The Highway and there he was hunched over a pair of draft. Ashtray between them. Smoke lazing up in the nicotine light. There was a dollar bill on the table between the beer glasses. He held the edge of it with the fingers of his left hand. Smoothed it out with the fingers of his right. He didn't own a nail clipper.

'You Al Delaney?'

He looked up. 'Depends who's askin'.'

I introduced myself. Told him what I'd heard, that he'd fought Joe Louis. 'That true?'

'That's what they say.'

He looked down. Tapped his cigarette and then turned the tip of it in the ashtray until it was sharpened, like a crayon. My move.

'Mind if I join you?'

'If you're doin' the buyin'.' He tapped a yellowed fingernail on the dollar bill. 'This here's my bankroll.'

'I'm buying.'

'Your choice of chairs.'

The waitress pulled up with a tray of draft on the upturned palm of her left hand. It was that kind of place. She made the rounds every few minutes with a full tray. You had to call her off if you didn't want any more. But you never had to crane around looking for her. Or call out. I dug for some cash and tipped her too much. She didn't smile, but she did say thanks. Al was watching my every move. He probably knew within five bucks how much money I had in my jeans. You could feel the hustle coming on. For the time being he didn't say anything. He just finished one draft and moved the empty aside and moved a fresh one into its place.

He drank from the one on his right. But he kept his left hand around the other. His cigarette had smoldered to death. I offered him one. He took two. One for now. One for above his left ear. He broke the filter off. I held out the match. He leaned the tip of his cigarette into the flame. But it was me he was watching the whole while. He was wearing one of those don't-turn-your-back looks.

'Why you wanna do a write-up on me now?'

I told him about the Bandit mentioning his name.

'My buddy the Bandit.'

'Everybody's buddy,' I said.

'If you got 30 cents for breakfast. Otherwise you're a bum.'

I told him I didn't know about him until the Bandit told me. I told him there'd be all kinds of people who'd never heard that story.

'You pay me for talkin'?'

I shook my head. 'Best I can do is beer and cigarettes.'

He thought about that while he finished the cigarette and the draft. He slid the empty over beside the other one and arranged his glasses so he had two empties on his left, two full ones on the right. I offered him another cigarette. He took two. One for his shirt pocket, one to light up. I did the honors. We sat there and smoked another cigarette apiece.

'I ain't too good on dates no more.'

I told him I didn't care about the dates.

'Names, neither.'

I told him I could work around that.

The waitress paid us another visit. Swapped full ones for the empties. While I was waiting for her to make change I took my notebook out of my jacket pocket. I put it on the table, near the edge. I tipped the waitress and pocketed the rest of the change. I took out my pen and put it on top of the notebook. Al watched all this with an air of detachment. But he didn't like it that the notebook and the pen were out on the table.

'My scrapbooks, pictures, all that stuff, it's in a trunk. Over at my brother's.'

I told him I could drive him over there.

He smiled. 'My brother's in 'Frisco. An' him'n me ain't talkin' just now.'

I shrugged, mouth and shoulders.

I told him we could get along without the notebooks. I told him it was what he remembered that I wanted to talk about.

There was another half-a-beer silence.

He took another cigarette. Just one this time.

I picked up my pen.

He looked at the notebook, then at me. 'I ain't said yes yet.'

'I haven't started writing yet.'

He still had a few of his teeth. They were about the colour of the first two fingers of his right hand.

The waitress arrived. Al held up his palm. 'Gotta go, sweetheart.' She looked at me. I shook my head. She turned and left. Not a word.

Al pushed his chair back a couple of feet. He finished the last of his beer. Stood up. He was more than six-three. Still pretty trim. 'I'll have to think about it.'

I asked him how long that might take.

He buttoned his overcoat and pushed his chair back toward the table.

'Meet me here tomorrow.'

'Same time?'

He nodded.

I followed him to the door.

He squinted against the sunlight, then smoothed his hair, left hand, right hand. He grabbed both lapels of his overcoat and gave his coat a shake, smoothed it out at the shoulders. He brushed his lapels. Left side. Right side. It was like he was going to meet a lady friend. Wanted to make himself presentable. He looked down at me, then out at the traffic, then down at me again.

'Ain't got a fin you could make the loan of?'

Next day, same waitress. Her name was Shirley. She put two drafts on the table without me having to ask. I gave her a couple of quarters. Told her to keep the change. 'Al Delaney been in?' She shook her head. 'Haven't seen him.'

A couple of guys were playing shuffleboard. Four guys were sitting, one to a table, along the far wall. They were all faced the same way. Like they were on a bus, going somewhere. The radio was tuned to a country station. Heartbreak and loss. None of them so much as tapped a toe. It was like they were all tuned in to their own personal station. That station didn't seem to be playing music. They drew on their smokes and sipped their beers and looked straight ahead. The only ones doing any talking were the ones playing shuffleboard. They cursed each other whenever one of them made a good shot.

Twelve-thirty and a whole crowd of guys came in together. They were laughing and joking and talking a little too loud. They were the centre of attention. They played to it. They were on lunch break from

42

somewhere. The waitress took one look at them and then turned to the bar. The bartender was already putting the glasses onto her tray.

I waited until half-past one. Except for one old guy in the corner, I was the only customer left in the place. I wanted to know if Al usually came in. 'He don't run like a clock.' She smiled. 'Two more?' I shook my head. She gave me one of those looks. Suit yourself.

*　　　*　　　*

'PUT THE TOP DOWN,' SAID ETHEL. SHE HAD BECOME 'ETHEL' THE afternoon I moved my stuff in and became her 'houseboy'. 'That button there.' She pointed with her cigarette in its tortoiseshell holder. Down went the top. 'I just love convertibles,' she said. 'I've always had one. There's something liberating about driving with the top down, don't you think?'

'Yes,' I said.

We were heading out to the airport. She was flying to Toronto, then on to New York, and from there to Cairo to begin her 'safari'. I still conjured up an image of her, cigarette, pith helmet and high heels atop a camel. I smiled.

'What are you smiling about?'

I told her.

She laughed. 'Well,' she said, 'believe it or not, I have been on a camel. An elephant as well. Our first trip to Africa, William and I both went on camels and, later, on elephants. I have the photographs to prove it. I must show them to you some time. Remind me.'

We were driving down Jefferson.

'We used to have all sorts of fun, the two of us. Did I tell you about our race to Georgia?'

'No,' I said. 'I'd have remembered that.'

'It was the summer of 1937. William had just bought us a pair of Ford convertibles, black for me, maroon for him. We headed south for a month's vacation. He could never stand being in the car while I drove—too fast for his liking—so we took our own cars. The first night we'd booked into a beautiful old hotel in North Carolina, The Grove Park Inn. A charming place right in the Blue Ridge Mountains.

We'd stayed there before and had vowed to go back. So off we went. I bet him a hundred dollars I'd beat him to the hotel. He may as well have given me the hundred before we pulled out of the drive.' She laughed, pulled the cigarette from its holder and tossed it overboard. 'I'd already checked in, had a bath and was on my second whisky when he arrived. He just shook his head, gave me a kiss, and handed over a hundred-dollar bill.'

We pulled in to the airport parking lot. I got out, opened the trunk, hauled out her suitcases, four of them, huge and heavy. Twenty minutes later, her luggage was checked in and Ethel had her ticket in her hand and there we were in the waiting area, waiting for her flight to be called.

'The Grove Park.' She smiled at the memory. 'It had a lovely verandah across the front. Big wicker chairs. A lovely view of the mountains. William and I were having a drink before going in to get dressed for dinner. Everyone dressed for dinners in those times. There was only one other person on the verandah, a young man sitting and drinking at a table at the far end. When the waiter came by, William told him to ask the young man if he wished to join us for a cocktail. We watched as the waiter conveyed the message. The young man looked at us and smiled, got up and came to join us.

' "That's very thoughtful of you," he said. "A pleasure."

' "He shook my hand, and then William's. "Scott," he said. We introduced ourselves and he sat down.

'A charming man. Very well turned out. And handsome. Elegant you'd have to say, suit and tie, polished shoes. Though he seemed rather sad. Or preoccupied. He asked us where we'd come from.

' "Canada," he said. "I have a friend, Ernest, who worked in Canada. Toronto. Back in the 20s."

' "Oh," I said. "What did he do?"

' "Worked for a newspaper," he said. "And what about you, William. What do you do?"

'My husband told him about his factory, the work he did for the automobile companies. "And you?"

' "I write," he said.

' "For newspapers?" said my husband.

' "No," he said. "Books. And, just now, scripts for the movies."

' "I don't believe I caught your last name," I said.

' "Fitzgerald."

' "*The Great Gatsby* Fitzgerald?"

' "Yes," he said.

' "Oh, my," I said. "And the Ernest you mentioned?"

' "Hemingway," he said.

' "Oh dear," I said, "I believe I'm going to faint."

'He laughed. "In that case, may I prescribe another of those?" He pointed at my glass.

'We ordered more drinks and my husband asked Scott what had brought him to North Carolina. "My wife," he said. "She's in a hospital here. I've come to visit her."

'It seemed indelicate to ask for details—it wasn't until we got home that William learned Zelda was in a mental institution in Asheville— and so we just settled in with our drinks and ...'

And just then a disembodied voice called her flight.

'Well, off I go,' she said.

'Have a wonderful time,' I said.

'Oh,' she said, 'I *will*.'

And off she went, Ethel into a robin's egg afternoon sky.

*　　　*　　　*

See? he said.

F. Scott Fitzgerald? Ernest Hemingway. Spare me. Really?

Really, he said.

*　　　*　　　*

WINDSOR'S AN OLD TOWN, AND ONCE UPON A TIME IT LOOKED IT. Downtown was all two and three-storey buildings, stores on the street level, walk-up flats above. It had department stores and hardware stores and grocery stores. You know, the kinds of things all cities used to have before someone came up with the hare-brained notion to build shopping centres and suck the life out of the heart of the city.

When I came to town, Devonshire Mall was still a glint in the eye of some developer somewhere. So downtown was still thriving. People came to shop. People came to eat in the fancy dining rooms at the Prince Edward Hotel and the Norton Palmer. They dropped in to Bartlett's and Smith's and Birks. They nosed in and out of the shops on Ouellette and Pelissier and Riverside Drive. Lots of traffic. Lots of bustle.

One of my favourite blocks was called Richmond Landing, which was one of the early names of what is now Windsor. It was a key block along Riverside west of Ouellette. And a few of my favourite places in Windsor were located right there: The Bandit's Café, Lee's, Gino's Italian Restaurant, South Shore Books and The Press Club.

Lee's was at the northwest corner of the block; The Press Club was on the second floor about midway in. The door to get up there was on Riverside—between Gino's restaurant on the west and The Paradise Chinese Restaurant on the east. Steep stairs—dangerous after a late night—which led to the upper door. Walk in and there was a big lounge area to your right with a series of river-facing windows. Turn left, go up a couple more stairs and you were in business: Shuffleboard along the east wall, bar along the west wall. And behind the bar was Val Dow. Val was maybe five-ten, five-eleven. Two hundred pounds or so. Built like a wrestler. His hands were half again as big as mine. You'd want to keep him smiling.

Val was a kind of surrogate father to all us young reporters. We loved Val. He could make any kind of drink you could imagine and several you'd never heard of. He was quick with a beer and quicker with a story. 'I ever tell you about the time Lester Pearson was in here?' 'The prime minister?' 'How many Lester Pearsons are there? Of course Lester Pearson the prime minister. Standing right about where you're standing. Remind me to tell you some time.'

Val knew most everyone worth knowing and many who weren't. And he allowed us to run a tab. Very comforting when you're making twenty bucks a week.

The Press Club was one of *the* places to be. It was lousy with reporters and photographers, of course. I think we paid five bucks a year to join. But it was also thick with politicians and lawyers, PR guys, cops, crooks and judges. They had to pay ten.

Memorable nights: Now and then a deck of cards would go flying, chairs would tip over, and Val would have to scurry out from behind the bar to separate the cheater from the cheated. Arguments were loud and long, sometimes several going on consecutively along the bar. If you got tired of the argument you were having, you could join the one next door. Occasionally, of course, a fist fight would break out. Entertaining, but rarely serious. Deep in the night, the fighters were not all that steady on their feet. One wild swing, missing the target entirely, and you'd find yourself down there on the carpet.

The young bucks would come in after work and stay until Val locked the doors. Have another one or two while he cleaned up and then leave along with him.

The older guys? Generally a few after work before heading home to the suburbs. But you could always tell when the wife had left town to visit her mother or the kids.

We hardly ever saw Bob Pearson at The Club. Bob was the Managing Editor. A pretty quiet guy. Usually. But when we saw him lingering at the bar, we knew his wife was gone for the week or the weekend, and we knew the last man standing was going to have to help him down the stairs, struggle him into the car, and then try to get him to give directions to his house.

'Vasey.'

'Yes.'

'Who said it's time to leave?'

'Val.'

'Really?'

'Yeah.'

'Why?'

'It's one thirty.'

'Really?'

'Really. Tell me again where you live.'

'I'm hungry. Let's get something to eat.'

'Sure.'

Off to The Paradise. Down the Press Club stairs, up the stairs to The Paradise. Say this about The Paradise. The only time you'd set foot in the place was when you were dead drunk, or the next thing to it. Have no idea what they served up. You could never tell, everything slathered in that orange sauce. But there were always interesting people in the booths. Long legs, short dresses.

'Had enough to eat?'

'Yeah.'

'Okay. Next stop, your house.' The trick—after getting his address—was just to drive. 'What the hell kind of car is this?'

'Coolest thing you've ever driven in.'

I fired up the Merc and off we went. After giving me vague directions, Bob nodded off, his head way back against the back of the seat, snorting and snoring. Took me a while to find the place, but we finally parked in the drive. I woke Bob and helped him out of the car, walked him up to his house, fished his keys out of his jacket pocket. Took me a minute to find the right one.

'Where are we?'

'Home.'

'Whose home?'

'Yours.'

'Who said I wanted to come home?'

'Well, we're here now. You may as well go in.'

'You know what, Vasey?'

'What?'

'You're fired.'

Luckily he forgot by the next morning.

*   *   *

A CITY THIS SIZE, THERE ARE ONLY SO MANY PLACES YOU CAN GO IF YOU'RE down to your last buck, newspaper stuffed in your shoes to keep your socks dry on account of the holes in your soles, thirsty. Bartenders' rule of thumb: Let one in, next thing you know the place is like a bus depot. Filled with gummers, legs crossed at the ankles, chins to chest, snoozing and snoring, keeping warm, waiting for Lady Luck to change her mind. I made the rounds: The Killarney, The Essex, The St. Clair, The B.A., back to The Highway, down to Lee's, over to Stanley's. I should've started with The Drake.

It looked like I was the last guy Al wanted to see. Me or the land-lord. As soon as he recognized me, he developed an intense interest in the soap opera on the television up in the corner of the room. I said hi. He seemed surprised to see me. 'Hey,' he said. 'Siddown.' The bartender looked at me. I looked down at Al. 'You want a couple more?' 'You still buyin?' I nodded. 'Sure.' I held up four fingers and sat down. The bartender set the beer on the bar. 'Here ya go, pal.' Self-serve. I got up, walked over, put four dimes on the bar, brought the beers over to Al's table.

We sipped and had a smoke. Al spent most of the time looking over my right shoulder at the television. It was like he was hoping I was going to drink up and shove off. When he started on the second draft, I took out my notebook and put it on the table. I put my pen on top of it. I told him I heard that one of his first instructors was Patsy Drouillard.

'Best fighter ever to come out of Windsor,' he said. 'Fought Billy Allen, an Ottawa kid, for the Canadian Lightweight Championship. Before I was born. 1910, 1911, somewheres in there. Broke both hands and still went twelve rounds. Lost on points.'

'You kidding?'

'I kid you not. Fought Allen again a year or so later and beat him. First Windsor fighter to win a national title. Held it for four or five years. Retired as champ. There's a fighter.'

I offered him another smoke. While I was lighting it, I asked him about Joe Louis.

'Ain't much to tell.' He drew on his cigarette and exhaled and laughed. It was a good laugh. The kind that makes you smile even if you didn't quite catch the joke.

'You really did fight him?'

'Sure I fought him. 1932, I fought him. I was sixteen when I fought him.'

I looked up from my notebook. 'I thought it was 1934.'

'Thirty-two. Thirty-four. I ain't so good on dates.'

'I thought you were eighteen when you fought him.'

'Coulda been. Sixteen. Eighteen.' He shrugged his eyebrows. 'Details, details.' He took another pull on his cigarette. He held it between his thumb and forefinger, cupped in his palm. He flicked the ash by tapping the cigarette with the nail of his little finger. 'I had the clap when I fought him.' Big laugh. It turned into a cough.

I pushed my chair back a little and set my notebook on my thigh. I wrote down what he'd just said. He didn't seem to like it, but he didn't object. 'The clap?' He grinned. It was a schoolboy's grin. Proud of something he oughtn't to be proud of. But a little defiant too. 'And me sixteen at the time.' I wrote it all down.

'Sixteen. Eighteen. Somewheres in there.'

The fight had taken place at the Detroit Naval Armouries. It was a big venue at the time. It was the kind of place where up-and-comers could get on a card with guys who'd won five or six fights, guys who were being talked about in New York and L.A. It was also the kind of place where people could make a few fast bucks if a kid from across the river knocked one of these guys on his can.

'My manager, he was a bootlegger. Carney Hall. Ever hearda him?' I shook my head. 'Yeah, well.' He took a last drag on his smoke and snuffed it. 'He was pretty big-time. Around here, anyways. May've been a hell of a bootlegger. But he didn't know dick about fightin'. If he had of, he'd never of put me in the ring with a guy like Louis.'

Al had gone four rounds. 'Not bad, eh? On two days' trainin'.' The bartender was all ears, elbows on the bar. I held up four fingers. 'I got a couple of shots in.' Bigger smile. 'I hit him so hard he put it in his book how hard I hit him.' He leaned back in his chair. I was writing everything down, but it didn't seem to bother him anymore.

' "Delaney carried the fight to me in the first couple of rounds. He hit me with a hard right which jolted me. I fought back with everything I had. I went right after him in the fourth round. I dropped him twice with lefts and finally with a left and a right to the head. He was a game fighter." ' Al drained his glass and put it on the table.

'You memorized that? From his book?'

'You kin look it up.' The bartender hadn't made a move toward the taps. I went back to my writing.

'Couple years later I met Louis on the golf links. He calls me over and says to the guy he's with "Can this guy hit? I got a hundred bucks for the fight and it cost me three hundred in dental work." '

The bartender was back at the taps. He set the glasses on the bar. I made a move to get up. He waved me off. He came round the bar and got the glasses and brought them over. I was digging in my pocket for change, brought out some coins. He shook his head. 'This round's on me.'

'Well, say,' said Al. He raised a glass to the bartender's health.

'You ever see him again? Joe Louis?' Al shook his head. I asked him about the fights he was in after that. But he had a detached look about him. Whatever he was thinking about, it was a private matter. I made a few more notes, then put the notebook on the table. It was still open. The pen was on top of it. I lit a cigarette. It was only when the match flared that Al looked at me.

'Say ...'

I gave him a smoke and lit it for him.

He drank one of the beers and started on the other. Then he pushed back from the table and stood. 'Gotta see a man about a dog.'

I went through my notes, adding things I remembered but which I hadn't had time to write down. Then I read them through again. I wrote a description of Al, what he was wearing, how he held his cigarettes. Then the news came on. There'd been a plane crash some-where down in the U.S. I turned my chair half-around so I could watch the report. They didn't know how many people had died, ex-actly. But no one had lived. It was about halfway through the newscast that I realized Al hadn't come back.

The bartender was leaning on the bar. He jerked his thumb over his shoulder. He did it a couple of times. 'Now you see him. Now you don't.' He grabbed a rag and started wiping the bar. I flipped my notebook closed and put it in my pocket. I picked up my smokes and matches and pen and stood up.

'Any idea where he might've gone?'

The bartender shook his head. 'Wherever he went, looks like he don't want you taggin' along.'

'Know where he lives?'

'Yup.'

By this time I was at the bar. He just looked at me. 'You goin' to tell me where?'

'He never tole ya, I shouldn't oughta.'

*   *   *

WINTERTIME, ONCE UPON A TIME SO THEY SAY, THE RIVER FROZE RIGHT OVER. This shore to that one. Completely. Back in Prohibition Days this was very handy for the rumrunners who were able to load up on our side and drive across to various cuts and canals and inlets on the American side, unload their cargo, grab the cash and head for home. Quick trip. Quick profit. Unless the ice gave way. In which case it was a quick trip to the bottom. Car, whisky and all. It's said, and who can say otherwise, that the river floor is littered with old jalopies and perfectly preserved bottles of Mister Walker's finest.

These days the river doesn't freeze over. Not completely, though from time to time there are floes jammed from shore to shore, the ice coming down from Lake St. Clair. The floes will pile up around Peche Isle, where the river is fairly narrow, and there are days when, standing by the railing downtown, the river appears pretty much ice-covered. Illusory: You wouldn't get far if you tried to walk over.

The ice makes a lovely tinkling sound as the current moves the floes and ice slush around. Mesmerizing as you stand watching. The gulls and ducks standing on the ice and getting a free ride down toward Lake Erie. The late-season freighters getting a mouth full of ice as they head upriver or down, leaving a swath of open water in their wake, the surface covered in a kind of mist-fog as the relatively warmer water meets the frigid winter air.

I love to go down by the bridge on those face-freezing winter days. There's a little pier sticking out into the river, parallel to the bridge. You're not supposed to go out there anymore. They've got it fenced off. However, out at the end you can look down and see the ice all piled up against the side of the pier and all around the massive cement footings of the bridge itself. Ice symphony, with a little bridge-traffic noise in the background.

A few years ago—November 2000—a painting crew was working on a platform suspended from the underside of the bridge. Then the platform let go. Four painters found themselves dangling from the bridge attached only by their safety harnesses before being hauled to safety nearly an hour later. Three others fell 130 feet into the river. Unbelievably, two of them were rescued. But 28-year-old Jamie Barker—stepfather of five and father of one—disappeared into the icy water. Barker's family kept a vigil along the Detroit River for ten days while crews removed nearly 30 tons of scaffolding from the river.

Nothing.

One of the cops said: 'He'll be found eventually, somewhere down the river.'

He was, five months later.

*   *   *

LUNCH IN THOSE DAYS WAS NOT SOMETHING YOU BROUGHT TO WORK IN A brown paper bag in your briefcase.

We didn't have briefcases.

Well, most of us didn't have briefcases. The only guy who did, the only one I remember, was Midnight Freddie, the overnight editor. Freddie was a little guy. Five-four or five. He had a big brown briefcase, the kind teachers used to have, the ones with a buckled leather strap and a rounded top that opens up. First thing he'd do when he got to work was put his briefcase on his chair, then go to the washroom and dampen some paper towel and give his work area the rub-down. Then he'd dry off the desktop with another piece of paper towel and get down for a desk-eye view, see everything was nice and clean. Then he'd place his briefcase on the desk, undo the buckle, open the top, then reach in and start pulling his stuff out and putting it on the desk. He did this standing up, which he had to do on account of his height. If he'd tried to do it sitting down he wouldn't have been able to see inside the briefcase. Even at that he was up to his elbow in the case.

First thing he'd bring out and plunk down on the desk was his Thermos. It was a big green one, about a foot tall, with a metal top which he'd unscrew and use as a coffee cup. One thermos would hold about a pot of coffee and last him the whole night. He couldn't stand the stuff that came out of the machine in the cafeteria. Who could blame him? Tasted like dishwater. Midnight was particular about his coffee. Hell, he was particular about everything. Once he got his Thermos situated, he'd bring out his pencils and ruler and glue pots and erasers. Midnight didn't like sharing stuff with others. There were pencils and rulers, rulers and erasers all over the place. Midnight never touched them. It was like he thought they could be contaminated with all kinds of nasty and potentially fatal germs. He took his stuff home at the end of the shift and brought it back the next day. We figured he probably wiped it off at home.

There was a place for everything on Midnight's desk. The Thermos went to his left. The pencils—six regular pencils, one black grease pencil, one red grease pencil—went to his right. He lined them up side by side, grease pencils on the outside. He laid his ruler out straight-ahead of him and put the gluepot in front of it. He put them all down in exactly the same order, in exactly the same place, every night of the week. He was death on disorder. Then he'd close the briefcase and put it on the floor beside his left foot. Come lunchtime, he'd lift it up, undo the buckle, open it up and bring out a tea towel which he used as a sort of tablecloth. He'd smooth it out, then bring out his food. He wrapped his sandwiches and cookies in tinfoil, two sandwiches and six cookies per shift. Midnight made his own sandwiches: One tuna, one peanut butter and jam. He wrapped each half individually. It was kind of a game to see which one he'd open first. 'Tuna!' he'd say. Always seemed to be a disappointment if the next half was also tuna. Ruined the suspense. Mrs. Midnight made the cookies. She was a killer cookie baker. But she seemed to have a limited repertoire. The cookies were always the same: Peanut butter. Chocolate chip. Oatmeal and raisin. Two of each. Individually wrapped.

Midnight was the exception when it came to lunches and briefcases

Like I said: Lunch wasn't something the rest of us would put in a briefcase. Even if we'd had one. Which we didn't.

Lunch was something you *did*. Sometimes very fancy. Sometimes not.

If we were in a hurry, we'd head to Kresge's lunch counter. Half the town ate there. They had big U-shaped counters—three or four of them jutting out from the main serving area. Comfy stools. Not your garden-variety stools—the kind you could twirl around on at the soda fountain—but very classy, with a little back to lean on and a nice footrest running all along the bottom, which Midnight would have loved if he'd ever gone there, which I doubt he did.

Basic stuff. But served up by nice waitresses who seemed to have a weakness for red lipstick and bunned-up hair they could stick their pencil into so they wouldn't lose it.

After you were there once or twice you were a regular. They'd recognize your face and give you a smile. Some of them even remembered our names.

'What'll it be, Hemingway?'

The food wasn't anything fancy. More or less home cooking, without the home. You could get a fish dinner with fried potatoes and a corn muffin for about 60 cents. Loved those corn muffins. Got one with your beef stew, too. Also 60 cents. If you were in a hurry you could grab a grilled cheese sandwich for a quarter. Coffee was a dime. Chocolate cake 15 cents a slice, 20 cents if you wanted a scoop of ice cream to go along with it.

No wonder the place was packed every day.

If you were lucky you'd find yourself sitting beside someone who was both hungry and chatty, and had something worthwhile to say.

For example. One day—this was a few months after I'd arrived in town—I settled myself on a stool and was studying the menu (it was a toss-up between grilled cheese, 25 cents, or a baked ham sandwich, 30 cents). The guy sitting next to me introduced himself. 'Anthony Quiller,' he said. I introduced myself, said it was nice to meet him. 'I've seen you over at the courthouse,' he said. I'd been covering courts the last couple of weeks. 'You're new?'

'Fairly new,' I said.

'You won't want for stories,' he said. 'There are more stories in this town than in *Aesop's Fables*. And the courthouse is a perfect place to find them.'

'What do you do there?'

'I'm a lawyer,' he said.

He asked me if I'd met Yorky.

I shook my head.

'You will.' He smiled.

'Yorky?'

'You'll see.' Anthony wiped his lips, scrunched up the paper napkin and dropped it on his plate. "Have to run. I'll see you around.'

'I expect,' I said.

He stood up, dropped a dime on the counter.

He smiled and he was gone.

'Didn't think the menu was that complicated.' The waitress was tapping her pencil on her order pad. And smiling.

'Grilled cheese,' I said.

'Anything else?'

I shook my head. 'Nope.'

I pulled my notebook out of my back pocket.

'Yorky.' I closed the notebook. Then I opened it again and wrote 'Anthony Quiller.' Closed it and put it back in my pocket.

Well, well, well.

So that was Kresge's.

If you had a little more time on your hands, and something of a thirst, Lee's was a pretty good bet.

Lee's was everyone's favourite. Very handy for those of us who lived at *The Star* at the time. We could drop in between deadlines, down a few, have a bite to eat and be back before anyone knew we were gone. Now and then, of course, we lingered a little longer. Why not? It was a very congenial place to spend an hour or more.

Walk in (the front door was off Riverside Drive, but there was a side door off Ferry Street which was closer if you were coming from *The Star*. Closer by maybe fifteen steps. Why waste time outside when you could be wasting time inside?). The interior was done up quite nicely in wood paneling. The floor was linoleum, black and white. The tables were little circular affairs, four chairs per. Our favourite nesting spot was the corner table just to your left as you came in by the side door. The corner featured a kind of triangular table with an L-shaped bench covered, like the chairs, in fake black leather. Very comfy. You could settle in there—six or seven of you on the bench and on the chairs—and apart from visits to the john (down the stairs—careful, steep stairs) you could easily spend an entire afternoon in conversation, thoughtful or otherwise.

Officially known as Lee's Imperial House, it was originally run by a chap named King Lee. King came to Canada back around 1914. He ran King's Café for a while and then the Savoy Café and then worked in the hotel which would later become known as Lee's Imperial House. This involved what you might call a change of fortune. King Lee and the hotel owner were chumming around down at the British American Hotel—northeast corner of Riverside and Ouellette—and found themselves in a friendly game of cards. King Lee's luck held. The hotel owner's did not. The owner ran out of money, but not nerve. He wanted to stay in the game. So he put his hotel in the pot, metaphorically speaking. King Lee won the card game and the hotel.

By the time I turned up in town, King Lee was long gone and the place was run by his sons: Pete, Ben and Jimmy. Terrific guys who loved what they did. They knew all their customers by name, knew where they worked (Post Office, *The Star*, the department stores over on Ouellette—Smith's or Bartlet MacDonald & Gow). They knew whether you liked your beers two at a time or not. Often as not, Pete or Ben would be pouring your beers as you walked in the door and setting them on the bar by the time you were wrestling the change out of your jeans.

The regulars received special attention.

There was a guy named George, a janitor over at Grace Hospital. George was a portly fellow. He owned the northwest corner of the bar. If someone came in before George arrived at his customary time and stood where George would shortly want to stand, Pete or Ben would set the fellow's beer a little further east on the bar. 'That spot's reserved.'

A spot at a beer-joint bar is reserved?

In this case, yes. Any other spot is all yours.

And in comes George. Ben is pouring one glass, then, without losing a drop, shifts the full glass out from under the tap and fills the second; places both glasses on the bar, which George grabs like handles on a lifeboat. George, like most of the rest of us, was a man of habit. He needed two glasses on the bar at all times. Full one on the left, working one on the right. As he approached the last taste of the glass on his right, he would slide that glass to the back of the bar, move his left-hand glass to the right and, at precisely that moment, Ben would slide another full one into his left hand. The Bolshoi couldn't have timed it more perfectly. And neither Ben nor George ever seemed to spill a drop. No one ever counted, but let's put it this way: George was never in danger of dying of thirst. He was a fixture at the bar long before I discovered Lee's, and he was in there every time I ever wandered in. I left town once—this would have been back in the 70s—for a stint in Toronto. George raised a glass to my good fortune as I teetered out after my going-away party. He raised his half-empty right-hand glass in welcome a couple of years later when I arrived back in town. 'You been on vacation?'

Time flies, George. Time flies.

Limited menu, but the beer was cold, plentiful and cheap (10 cents a glass the year I moved to town. You could get yourself in an awful lot of trouble for a buck). The menu, as I recall, was pretty basic. There were pickled eggs, which I never ate. There were also pig's knuckles (disgusting looking in their big jar behind the bar). And there were sandwiches. This is before the advent of microwave ovens. So if you wanted your sandwich heated up, Pete or Ben would slide it into a little toaster oven. It would come out too hot to handle for a minute, with the cellophane wrapper all crinkly and burnt at the edges. I'm thinking ham and cheese: The cheese now all runny and the bread soggy from the melted cheese. After three or four beers, it was haute cuisine. And you rarely left Lee's before having downed three or four beers. (Small glasses, as I recall. Those skinny little ones that bulged out a bit at the top).

I remember covering a drunk driving case one time. Judge Gordon Stewart presiding. The Crown was outlining the facts of the case: Erratic driving concluding in an unfortunate event with a tree. The driver tumbling out and stumbling about. He'd come from a roadhouse down the way. 'Our best guess is that he consumed twenty glasses of beer prior to encountering the tree,' said the Crown.

'Twenty glasses of beer?' said an incredulous Stewart. 'No one could drink that much and live to tell about it.'

The Judge was a real joker. He'd probably have ten with his lunch.

There were some other great spots downtown, and we made a point of investigating most of them.

The Radio Tavern was up on Ouellette, near Wyandotte. One of the world's great bars. Dark and quiet. Or the bar at the Norton

Palmer Hotel: Long and narrow, on the Pelissier Street side. Very comfy. And if you were hungry you could zip down to the basement restaurant and get one of Mrs. Norton's famous meat pies.

There was a piano bar, down on Ouellette near Riverside, the name of which escapes me. Great little hideaway. Go down the stairs and there on the right was the piano, and the bar. Go through the doorway and there was the dining room.

One day a bunch of us—Karen Hall and I forget who else—went down for a late lunch, 1:15 or so in the afternoon. And whom should we discover sitting at the bar but Jack Kent. Jack had been a major during the Second World War. Very famous: Prisoner-of-war and so forth. The Major was *The Star*'s business editor. You would rarely find him at *The Star*. You could always find him in one bar or restaurant or another chatting up some businessman or another. As they say, news doesn't happen in the newsroom. But it drove the City Editor crazy. In the days before cell phones he never knew how to find the Major.

Once—I'm almost sure I've got the details right—*The Star* hired a new City Editor. The new guy decided he needed to set an example, get everyone to sit up and pay attention to him.

He took one look at the Major and thought, there's my man.

The Major's routine went something like this: He'd show up at 10:30 or 11, go to his desk, sit down, pick up the receiver, dial a number, then recline so far back in his chair you were certain he was going to tip right over backwards. 'Hello,' he'd say. And within five minutes he'd have lunch all set up. He'd lean forward, replace the receiver, fiddle around with the junk on his desk, then get up and head for the door. Sometimes he came back before everyone else had left for the day.

The new City Editor was going to put a stop to all that. He told Jack to show up at 9, no later, spend the morning at his typewriter, take a one hour lunch and so forth. The Major, leaning back in his chair, hands clasped over his ample belly, listened, nodded and, when the City Editor was done, sat back up, picked up the receiver, dialed, leaned back and made arrangements for lunch. The City Editor hollered out as he was heading for the exit. At his age, the Major could have been hard of hearing.

He showed up next morning right on time—a shade before 11—and the City Editor was all over him like flies at a picnic. 'I told you ...' and so forth. Another warning. Another warning ignored. So when the Major showed up next day, right around 11 or so, the City Editor told him he was fired. The Major didn't say a word. Sat down, picked up the receiver, dialed ...

'Didn't you hear me?'

The Major held up his index finger, spoke into the phone. 'Mario's? Twelve o'clock? Wonderful. See you there.' And off he went.

The City Editor was beside himself. He stormed in to Norm Hull's office. Told his sad story. Norm listened for about a minute, then stood up. 'You did what?'

'Fired him.'

'You can't fire the Major. The only person in this building who could fire him is me, and if I did that the publisher would fire me. He's an institution.'

'I already did fire him.'

'Well go unfire him. Now!'

'He's gone for lunch.'

'Where'd he go?'

'I think he said Mario's.'

'Well get your ass up there. And when you're done unfiring him, apologize. Tell him it'll never happen again.'

Which he did. Which was why the Major would continue to enjoy afternoon-long lunches until the day he retired.

Which brings us back to the piano bar. The Major looked around as we came down the stairs. 'Well, who do we have here?'

'In for a late lunch, Major. Care to join us?'

'Well, that would be just fine.'

He got off his bar stool and followed us into the dining room.

'Another martini, Major?' said the bartender.

'Yes. Please.'

So we all sat down and the waitress brought the menus and, a few minutes later, a round of beer. And then the bartender arrived with a little tray. A martini glass and a pitcher, one of those small beer pitchers, filled to the brim. 'Here's your martini, Major.'

'That's a martini?'

'That it is. And that's why I patronize this fine establishment.'

'How many is that?'

'Impertinent,' said the Major. 'But if you must know, this is my second. I try to limit myself during office hours.'

*   *   *

Did this really happen? she said
Some of this happened, he said.
The rest of it? she said.
Should have, he said.
How much of this is true?
All of it, he said.

*   *   *

MRS. MAJOR WIGLE WAS HEAD OF THE HISTORICAL SOCIETY. HEAD OF *The Hysterical Society* was the way the City Editor sometimes referred to her, but only after he was certain she'd actually left the newsroom. Mrs. Major's real name was Cora, but no one called her that. Everyone, including Cora herself, called her Mrs. Major. Her late husband had, like Jack Kent, been a major during the Second World War. Very famous: Injured, prisoner-of-war, much-decorated and so forth. Unlike Jack, he did not live to tell the tale. Nevertheless.

Anytime Mrs. Major Wigle felt one of the city's architectural gems was being threatened she would call the City Editor and tell him she was on her way down to *The Star* with some information that would come in handy *when* he assigned one of his reporters to write the story. And she, of course, would be willing to be interviewed.

'I should be there in ten minutes.'

And ten minutes later, Geoffrey, her aged chauffeur, would pull the 1947 royal-blue Cadillac limousine to the curb, hobble around to the passenger side all gussied up in his black uniform and matching cap, open the door for her eminence, reach in and help hoist her out. The wags used to say Mrs. Major ought to be driving Geoffrey, since he seemed to be about ten years older than she was. This was said in a whisper, of course.

So, many memorable things about Mrs. Major. But I'd say the *most* memorable thing about her—apart from her rings and necklaces and earrings and bracelets and her light-blue hair—was her enthusiasm when it came to the history of Windsor. She had the unfortunate habit of clasping her hands as a sort of exclamation point after telling you an important fact or detail. She was fond of superlatives. She was the kind of woman whom it is easy to mimic. But you felt bad after you did the mimicking.

Anyway, one day she bustled up the stairs and across the newsroom and presented herself in front of the City Editor's desk. This was, it seems to me, right around deadline time. Sparks were flying from the City Editor's pipe as he hollered at someone to change the headline on the fire story. Then he removed his pipe and did his best to smile at Her Eminence. 'What can I do for you, Mrs. Major?'

'What you *may* do,' she said with a sweet smile, 'is assign one of your reporters to do a story about Colonel Prince.'

'He still dead?'

'Yes, of course.'

'So the angle would be?'

'We're hoping to have the government put up a plaque in his honour.'

'Why now?'

'Why not?'

The City Editor looked around. I was making a run for it—heading to the hallway leading to the cafeteria. 'Hemingway. C'mere.'

Which is how you get to be an expert in matters pertaining to the late great Colonel Prince. Mrs. Major gave me the lowdown as we sat in the cafeteria. The interview went, approximately, an hour and a bit.

The short version:

Colonel John Prince was a lawyer in his native Hereford in England, emigrating to Canada in the early 1830s with his wife, four children, five servants and reputedly a box containing thousands of gold coins so heavy it took two men to lift it. He used part of his little fortune to buy a 200-acre estate in what was then Sandwich, now part of West Windsor, bordered on one side by what is now known—aptly enough—as Prince Road.

He resumed his legal career and became an officer in the Essex Militia.

Mrs. Major thought him quite the fellow. Smart, a good lawyer, tough and 'a little bit crazy.' He was not, she thought, the type of man you'd want to annoy. She offered this tale, by way of proof.

Prince had his friend Doctor Hume over for breakfast one December morning in 1838 when a messenger arrived at the house to report that a couple of hundred Americans were invading Windsor. The Colonel, dressed in hunting attire, buckled on his sword and rode off to raise his troops. The doctor went looking for the wounded.

The invaders, who called themselves Patriots, wanted to make Upper and Lower Canada a republic, thus freeing the inhabitants from life under the rule of people like Prince. Their foray ended badly. Prince's militia killed 21 of the invaders and captured four. The rest hightailed it back across the river.

After the rout, Colonel Prince came across the body of Doctor Hume. One arm hacked off and a bayonet had been thrust through his chest. His body was being eaten by hogs in the pigpen where the invaders had tossed it.

Enraged would not adequately describe the Colonel at this moment.

Shortly afterward, Prince came across the members of his militia who had taken four of the invaders prisoner. Prince ordered the Americans shot on the spot. He said they were nothing more than pirates and, as such, were liable for execution without trial. Critics thought this a little excessive and demanded an explanation. The Colonel obliged: 'I ordered them to be shot and it was done accordingly.'

Rebel sympathizers in Detroit put a bounty on Prince, dead or alive. Prince countered with advertisements in Detroit newspapers alerting would-be bounty hunters there were numerous hidden traps and spring guns throughout his estate.

No attempts were made on his life.

A military inquiry cleared him of any wrongdoing, and his actions were defended in the British House of Lords by the Duke of Wellington, then Prime Minister. Although some were appalled, many applauded him. Some have suggested his brutal treatment of the prisoners put an end to the Patriots' desire to invade Windsor again.

Prince was, in many circles, a very popular fellow. He was referred to in the press as 'the King of the western district, if not Upper Canada.' Not surprisingly, when he decided to run for the Upper Canada General Assembly, he was elected. And re-elected. And spent 18 years as the representative from Essex.

Many years later—1860—Attorney-General John A. Macdonald appointed Prince the first judge of Algoma District, and Prince, then 64 years old, moved to Sault Ste. Marie, which was not yet incorporated as a village. Despite having angled for the appointment, Prince was not a fan of the location: 'I think the Soo a wild and horrid and inhospitable place ...' His opinion of the place never changed much. 'Bothered very much by the heathens in this accursed Soo, and parts adjacent,' he would write prior to his death.

His wife apparently shared his view of the north. When he headed north, she and three of the children remained in Sandwich. Only Prince's youngest son went with him, and a few years later he left for pastures less bleak, leaving Prince to spend the rest of his life alone and in ill health and, it seems, ill humour. As a judge he was considered unpredictable, frequently bending the law in favour of what he considered real justice, and it is said that he ruled with an iron hand.

Within a year of his arrival, Prince had set himself up on a 128-acre river-side estate, built a two-storey waterfront residence, Belle Vue Lodge, where he lived from 1861 until his death in 1870. He was buried a few hundred feet from Belle Vue Lodge '... in the accursed soil must rest and rot my miserable remains and on that solitude island opposite, for I will not allow my dust to mingle with the human race, whom I hate.'

He willed the estate to his housekeeper.

Part of the estate is now a municipal park and, fittingly, (Mrs. Major would have been delighted) there's a plaque commemorating the Colonel. Here's what it says:

> Here, on a portion of his former estate, is buried Col. Prince who emigrated from England in 1833 and settled at Sandwich, Upper Canada. As commanding officer of the Essex Militia, he

stirred up a violent controversy by ordering the summary execution of four members of an armed force sympathizing with Mackenzie's Rebellion which invaded the Windsor area from Detroit in December, 1838. He represented Essex in the legislative assembly 1836-40 and 1841-54. Prince was appointed the first judge of the Algoma District in 1860. Colourful and eccentric, he became one of early Sault Ste. Marie's best known citizens.

Colourful and eccentric.

Yeah.

If you'd like to see what he looked like, that can be arranged.

See if you can get one of the curators to take you to the basement of the Baby House museum. Ask to see the Colonel's head. It's there in a cardboard box.

Well, a plaster bust of it.

Creepy. But worth a look.

And Mrs. Major got her plaque, too. It's outside the Baby House museum, and it tells the story of the invasion of Windsor and Colonel Prince ordering the summary execution of the 'pirates'. And if you snoop around the little cemetery on Wyandotte Street West at Huron Line you just *might* find the grave where those 'pirates' are buried.

*   *   *

HERE'S ONE I'D NEVER HEARD BEFORE, COURTESY OF MY PAL TOM LUCIER.

'Another one from my father. If there was a body missing in the river, there was apparently a ceremony designed to help find it. They'd get a loaf of bread and have a priest bless it. Then they'd toss the loaf into the river and watch the loaf float along. Where it stopped was apparently where they'd find the body.'

You usually don't need the loaf.

Hard to say how many people have killed themselves in the river. Two or three a year, I'd say. Three or four days, or a couple of weeks or a month or two later, the bodies wash ashore somewhere downriver. If they've been in the river any length of time, fishing them out is not something you'd want to find yourself doing.

Some of the stories lodge themselves in memory.

A FEW YEARS AGO, EIGHT OR TEN, ONE SUNNY SUMMER DAY, A WOMAN TOOK her two young sons to Belle Isle. She took the boys by the hand and walked into the river. One of them fought his way free and watched as his mother and little brother disappeared beneath the surface.

Police pulled the mother and younger brother from the river. The little boy—five or so—died on the beach while officers tried to revive him. The mother was taken to the hospital, where she too died. The little survivor, quoted in *The Detroit Free Press*: 'Why did Mommy do this?'

Then this, four or five years ago: A man drove his black Chevy SUV to Belle Isle, pointed it toward the river, revved the engine, took his foot off the brake. Police divers found the vehicle, and the driver, in eight feet of water.

And just the other day: Windsor police pulled the body of a 44-year-old rest home resident from the river. He had been missing for ten days. Two passersby spotted the body at the edge of the river in the 7500 block of Riverside Drive East—where the man asked a taxi driver to drop him off the last time he was seen alive.

Every time you read one of these stories you wonder: *What would that be like?* To jump off a breakwall, to rev your vehicle to the limit and take your foot off the brake. Walk your kids into the river.

Desperate.

Some do so in plain sight in the middle of the day. More an SOS than a heartfelt attempt. But those who are serious make sure no one is looking or close enough to haul them out.

What I wonder about is that final stretch, when you're too weak to fight any more, and you just let yourself be pulled under. A relief, I guess, if you were really serious in the first place. But I can't help but think that some of them would have a horrifying final few seconds, having changed their minds, struggling—fighting finally and too late, too far out, too weak, the current too strong and relentless—to save themselves.

Not something you want to think about for more than a moment or two.

*   *   *

THEN THERE ARE THE PEOPLE WHO JUMP INTO THE RIVER AND REALLY shouldn't come out. Alive. But now and then they do.

Just last month *The Windsor Star*'s Trevor Wilhelm blogged that a 47-year-old guy named John Morillo had a few beer (eight according to one count) then decided it would be a terrific idea to jump into the river and swim to Detroit. And back.

You might ask, as any reasonable (and sober) person might: John, what on earth were you thinking?

Trevor asked and got this response.

'I was drinking, but I wasn't really drunk,' Morillo said. 'The thing is, I've been telling people I'm going to swim across the river for years and they're like "yah, yah, blah, blah, you can't make it." So, I don't know, last night I just decided it was the time to go.'

Fuelled, as they say, but perhaps not firing on all cylinders. A view shared by his mother, once she heard about his exploits. 'She just hung up on me,' Morillo told Trevor. 'She said "you're just so stupid." '

A view Morillo apparently shared. 'Shortly after getting out of jail Tuesday,' Trevor blogged, 'Morillo admitted he's "really stupid" and regrets causing a hassle for authorities, but added he didn't expect it would cause such a stir.'

It did, of course.

He began his little cross-border adventure down near the Hiram Walker complex and claimed he swam sort of diagonally to the Renaissance Center. And then?

'When I got to the Renaissance Center,' he told Wilhelm, 'I couldn't find a way to get up onto the platform,' said Morillo. 'Then some guy said "Hey, there's a ladder over here." I climbed up the ladder, then people were asking to take their pictures with me. There was one woman, she said she was from Windsor and she thought I was crazy. She was right.'

Then he slipped back in the river for his return trip. It wasn't long after that he realized his swim had attracted more attention than anticipated.

According to Wilhelm's blog: 'Morillo's neighbour, who wanted to witness his swim, called police about half an hour after he jumped into the river when she lost sight of him. Windsor police responded to the 1600 block of Riverside Drive around 11:30 PM. Police notified the Canadian and U.S. coast guards. Three boats and a helicopter were deployed to search the area. The U.S. coast guard found Morillo around 12:50 AM, swimming on the Canadian side just west of the Hilton hotel.'

'As soon I saw the helicopters going by and the boats looking for me,' he told Wilhelm, 'I was like "Oh, this is really stupid." ' He said he was just about to climb back on shore in Windsor when officers came up in a boat and told him to get out of the water.

Once he hauled himself ashore in Dieppe Gardens, Morillo was charged with being intoxicated in a public place. Police said the Windsor Port Authority was also investigating and would be contacting Transport Canada. 'Morillo said Windsor's harbour master told him he'll likely be fined for swimming in a shipping channel, which could run anywhere from $5,000 to $25,000.'

And then, of course, people began to wonder if he'd really made it all the way across and back again. Or whether he'd just dog paddled from Hiram Walker's to Dieppe Gardens.

Remember Toad? '… much that he related belonged more properly to the category of what-might-have-happened-had-I-only-thought-of-it-in-time-instead-of-ten-minutes-afterwards.'

Like Toad of Toad Hall, Morillo was injured by the mere suggestion. He told Wilhelm: 'If I'm going to be in the paper, I'd at least like them to say I actually made it, even though I got in trouble and everything. I gotta pay fines and stuff. But I don't want it to sound like I didn't make it, because then my buddies are going to say "Ha, ha, you didn't make it." Because that was the whole thing, to show them I could do it.'

Lo and behold.

A week later, Dalson Chen blogged in *The Windsor Star*: 'There's finally photographic evidence that Windsor's John Morillo really did swim clear across the Detroit River and back again. Images provided to *The Star* appear to show the 47-year-old Canadian emerging from the water at the Renaissance Centre on the Detroit side of the border. Markus Wolfstetter, a passerby, said he took the pics, including one showing him side-by-side with Morillo, on the night of July 22. Wolf-stetter described Morillo as "slightly drunk, but extremely cordial, and more amused with himself than proud." '

Wolfstetter told Chen: 'He seemed to have no interest in fame. We repeatedly asked if we could contact someone on the other side to verify he had made it. He said he didn't need the attention, and was satisfied proving it to himself.'

And then, of course, doubts began to emerge about the authenticity of the photos in question.

Note Dalson Chen's phrasing:

'Images provided to *The Star* appear to show the 47-year-old Canadian emerging from the water …'

But hey, let's not allow a few doubts to get in the way of a good story.

It is after all, as Toad would acknowledge, a very good story.

*   *   *

YORKY TURNED OUT TO BE A LITTLE GUY. REALLY LITTLE. LITTLER THAN Midnight Freddy. Five-foot-two. Five-three, tops. A hundred pounds, maybe. Even with a full wine bottle in his pocket. White hair, thick-lensed glasses, just a hint of the home country on his tongue. He wore a beige trench coat. Well, it had been beige once upon a time.

He came up before Judge Gordon Stewart. Always, apparently. Gord was a kind of pal, in a weird way (he would be one of Yorky's pallbearers). Gord being known to have a drink himself, sometimes several, during his lunch break at The Top Hat after having sentenced Yorky to another stint in the jail down on Sandwich Street. 'Drunk in a public place' for the most part.

Stewart, and most of the lawyers, always went for lunch at the Top Hat. Pretty swank place, once upon a time. The time had passed. By the time I started following Stewart in there for a mostly liquid lunch, your shoes kind of stuck to the carpet. Nice and dark, though, and a good distance from prying eyes. We—the reporters and lawyers and court officials—all kept an eye on the judge in order to know when to drink up and head back to work. Stewart was not often in a hurry to get back to the bench, which explained why His Honour sometimes seemed to nod off during afternoon proceedings.

Anyway, Yorky was led in from the holding cells to the prisoners' box looking the worse for wear—hair at all angles, clothes wrinkled and stained, glasses askew. He looked the way a Labrador retriever will when he accidentally poops on the basement floor. Remorse doesn't quite encompass it. I didn't even know him and I felt like going over and giving him a hug.

The court clerk called his name—'Norman Haworth'—and he stood up, both hands on the rail before him. Doleful look in those watery eyes. No wonder Stewart didn't look at him.

The clerk read out the details.

'On or about 2 PM, Saturday the …'

Yorky hung his head.

Stewart was staring at the ceiling.

The radio reporter sitting next to me leaned over and whispered: 'I think this is appearance number 338.'

'Three hundred and thirty eight?'

'I'm pretty sure. Once it got over three hundred, the Crown started keeping track. They're thinking he may make the *Guinness Book*.' She smiled a grand-daughterly smile.

So, three hundred and thirty eight and counting. The details were always the same: Yorky drunk and causing a disturbance (shouting and swearing); Yorky drunk and sleeping in the bus depot. If the details were particularly embarrassing—Yorky urinating on an officer's foot, let's say—he would hold his head in his hands.

Sometimes, to the astonishment of everyone in the room, he would express surprise at the details just read out by the clerk, claiming it was entirely out of character, and that he had never found himself in such a low circumstance in his entire life. It was all Stewart could do not to smile.

'Is that it?'

'More or less, Your Majesty.'

Today, nothing special. Yorky drunk and sleeping it off in the mouth of the railway tunnel down by the riverfront. The railway police had found him. Called the cops. The cops had come and carted him off.

'Mister Haworth?'

Yorky looked up.

Stewart looked down. 'Do you have anything to say for yourself before sentence is passed?'

Yorky looked directly at the judge. 'I would just like to say how embarrassed I am to have been found in such a sorry state, Your Majesty. I would like to apologize to you, Your Majesty, and to society in general. I would like you to know I am undertaking to mend my sorry ways, turn a leaf in the repetitious story of my life and endeavour to become a new and better and more respectable ...'

'Very well, Mister Haworth. That'll do.'

Yorky looked at the judge. Then he looked at his hands gripping the rail of the prisoner's box. Then he looked back up at the judge.

Depending on his mood—and perhaps on how much he'd had to drink at The Windsor Club the night before—Stewart might offer a good tongue-lashing, saying what a scourge Yorky was, what a threat to public decency and so forth. But usually he would look down at the paperwork before him and then thump his gavel and pronounce sentence. Ten days. Fifteen days. Seven days. Whatever number popped into his head.

He thumped his gavel.

'Five days,' he said. 'And I wish you well in your attempt to turn a page in the story of your life.'

Yorky looked up at the judge.

The judge looked down at Yorky.

'Your Majesty?'

'Yes.'

'Would you mind looking at your calendar?'

Stewart looked at Yorky, then looked down at his day planner.

'Oh,' he said, looking up at Yorky. 'I'm sorry, Mister Haworth. I lost track.' He thumped his gavel. 'Thirteen days,' he said.

Thirteen days being the number of days remaining in the month and the number of days before Yorky's pension cheque arrived.

'Thank you, Your Majesty.'

'You're quite welcome, Mister Haworth. Next.'

Yorky offered the judge a big smile and off he went, through the doorway and off to jail. It was always a pleasant trip. As Anthony

Quiller would later tell me, a trip to jail was for Yorky like going home. In fact, it was his home: He gave the jail address as his home address. And thus it was that all his mail—pension cheques especially—arrived there and was kept for him until he showed up. If for some astonishing reason he was not sent there for a few days' rest at the end of the month, he would have to trudge down and knock on the door and ask for his mail. Rare was the month that happened.

He was always taken to the same cell, not too far from the guards' station. The cell door was never locked. After lights out he would pad out of his cell and join the guards in a friendly game of Crazy 8s at the lunch table. During the day he would keep himself busy with odd jobs—sweeping, washing dishes. Pretty cozy. He got to have warm showers and get his laundry done. He had three squares a day and a warm bunk at night. All in all, who could ask for anything more?

'They even pack him a lunch on the day of his release,' said Anthony. 'And, of course, they hand him his pension cheque.'

*　　*　　*

AROUND TWO IN THE MORNING, LARRY AND I WERE AT OUR USUAL POSTS, feet up on the radiators, coffee mugs in hand, though not much coffee mixed in with the whisky.

'What's that smell?' I said.

'That smell?' said Larry. 'That's what you're drinkin' my man.'

You can always tell you're in a distillery town.

There's no smell quite like it. 'Excellent,' as Larry would say. Sweet and yeasty and when the wind is blowing from the east you can smell Hiram Walker's distillery all the way to the open newsroom windows in downtown Windsor, which, once upon a time, was a separate town. The distillery being, of course, in Hiram's own town, which he named Walkerville, modesty not being one of his strong suits.

'There's a guy you should read up on,' said Larry.

I had a better idea.

Next day I dialed the phone. 'Mrs. Major? I wonder if you'd help me out.'

Half-an-hour later Geoffrey pulled the ancient Caddy to the curb, got out and opened the door for me. I joined Mrs. Major in the back seat. The back seat—grey velour with little grey braided-rope hand straps hanging from the window frames—was so far back you could stretch out your legs and still not touch the back of the front seat. There was a little mahogany table behind the front seat with holes in the top. A crystal decanter in the centre hole. Crystal glasses in the smaller holes to either side.

'For show only, these days,' said Mrs. Major.

Though the original owner—a funeral home operator she wouldn't care to name—always had the decanter filled—and refilled—with Hiram Walker's finest.

Fitting.

For the next hour or so, as Geoffrey took us on a trip down the Drive and into the heart of Olde Walkerville, Mrs. Major took us on a trip to the last century.

Like most of us, Hiram came from somewhere else. In his case, East Douglas Massachusetts, then Detroit and then, thanks to Upper Canada's lax liquor laws, across the river in 1856. Windsor wasn't much to speak of back then, just a little town on the river with a population of about a thousand. But just east of town there was a lot of vacant land, and Hiram bought up about 500 acres extending back from the river to what is now Tecumseh Road.

The riverfront land was perfect for a distillery—access to the water and markets east and west in an expanding British Empire—and the rest of it was just what he needed to build himself a town.

Within a dozen years his distillery was the biggest in Canada. And within twenty years, his town was one of the finest in the country, with 600 cottages built for his workers, and amenities which were the envy of those living elsewhere: Everything from paved streets with street lights, running water from its own pumping station, its own police force and fire department, all paid for by Uncle Hiram.

He brought in the best architects and planners he could find and created a model community. 'And he owned and controlled it all,' said Mrs. Major. And since he owned the land and the cottages, he could control who lived there, and those who lived there were, of course, the people he hired to work in his distillery in his little company town. And then, just to make sure Windsor didn't try to amalgamate it (the city would, but long after Hiram had gone to his grave), he had Walkerville incorporated as an independent town.

So, Hiram succeeded in building a hugely successful business and a little fiefdom. Strangely, after only a brief stint in Walkerville in its earliest days, he returned to Detroit, where he lived until his death. He took a ferry to Windsor each morning, then drove along the river to his distillery. Eventually he tired of the commute. In 1880 he leased a ferry named *Essex*, built a dock at the foot of (what else?) Walker Street in Detroit and another in front of his distillery across the river, and thus saved a lot of time and hassle by making his way directly to and from work in elegant fashion. 'That,' said Mrs. Major, 'was the beginning of the Walkerville and Detroit Ferry Company, which continued to operate until 1942. Remind me to tell you more some time.'

Business continued to boom, which did not escape the attention of Hiram's American rivals. The booze barons petitioned friendly lawmakers in Washington—perhaps over a few drinks?—for a little protection, and the lawmakers passed legislation requiring importers of whisky to identify their products by country of origin. Good idea, thought Hiram. 'Which is why,' said Mrs. Major, 'Canadian Club is called Canadian Club.' And Canadian Club became much more popular than Walker's Whisky ever had been.

The empire grew and grew. In 1894 Hiram Walker spent a small fortune ($100,000 dollars at the time) to build a palatial head office right there on the waterfront. We were parked right out front, in a no-parking zone, cars honking as they went past. 'It's modeled after the Pandolfini Palace in Florence,' said Mrs. Major, 'with interiors by the world famous Albert Kahn.' And the walls alive with paintings by the Group of Seven and other famous Canadian artists which Mrs. Major pointed out as we wandered the halls while Geoffrey was out front in his no-parking zone, ignoring angry passersby.

'Go up here, Geoffrey,' said Mrs. Major. Geoffrey hung a left and then a right, and Mrs. Major pointed out the rowhouses, left and right. 'These were for the workers. Still charming,' she said. 'And turn right here, Geoffrey.' Have you seen Willistead? I shook my head. 'Well,' she said, 'you're in for a treat. It's something very special.'

I was. And it was.

RIGHT THERE IN THE HEART OF OLDE WALKERVILLE STANDS A MANOR HOUSE like you see in British tourist brochures, built by Hiram Walker's second son Chandler. 'It was designed by Albert Kahn,' said Mrs. Major. 'Took them two years to build,' she said. 'They finished it in 1906.'

'Why Willistead?'

'It's named after Chandler's late brother Willis.'

'Impressive,' she said. 'Beautiful inside. We'll have to take a tour one day. All those rooms, and only one bedroom.'

'One?'

'Chandler and his wife had no children. So they didn't need a lot of bedrooms.'

'Didn't they have any friends who came to stay for the weekend?'

'They stayed in the guest house,' said Mrs. Major.

'Of course,' I said.

'Would you like to go around the block again, ma'am,' said Geoffrey, eyeing us in the rear-view mirror.

'No,' said Mrs. Major. 'You can take us back to *The Star*.'

'Right ma'am.'

I took one last look at the place. 'Sort of like a little castle for a little prince,' I said.

'The Walkers were as close to royalty as you'll get around here,' said Mrs. Major. 'And they certainly thought of themselves that way. Particularly Hiram. He made bags and bags of money. What he wanted he bought or got, and he ran it all as though he were king of the world. And he was. At least this little corner of it.'

'When did he die?'

'He died in 1899. He was 94.'

If you want to visit his grave, you'll have to cross the river. He's buried in the Elmwood Cemetery in Detroit.

'Would you like to see it?' said Mrs. Major.

'Perhaps some other time.'

'Well, just let me know. Geoffrey will take us. Whenever it's convenient.'

'Sounds great,' I said.

'Have you been along the river. LaSalle? Amherstburg?'

'Not yet,' I said.

'Well, we must take a tour. Lots of history down that way.'

'That'd be great.'

'I'll call you,' she said. 'We'll set something up.'

*   *   *

SO THAT WAS WALKERVILLE.

Much later, in the '80s, I came to know, and grew to love, another place. At the other end of the social scale—and the other end of town—was a little riverfront community called Brighton Beach. Gone now. Houses torn down, residents scattered who knows where.

Walkerville has its distillery.

Brighton Beach had Zug Island.

All kinds of reasons to go to Walkerville. Not so many to go to Brighton Beach. Unless you heard a call on the police scanner, which is how I made my way down there the first time. Someone had found a body in a field down by the river. Not the first time this had happened, apparently. People saw it as a kind of perfect area to get rid of what they no longer wanted hanging around—old toilets, chairs and sofas, and all kinds of other junk. And bodies.

This one turned out to be a dead hooker. But we would have to wait a day or so to find that out.

We zipped out Riverside Drive past the bridge—Cecil Southward, the photog doing the driving (the photogs always seemed to do the driving, like the staff cars were theirs and theirs alone).

'This should prove to be interesting,' said Cec. 'You been to Dogpatch yet?'

'Dogpatch?'

'That's what they call it.'

We wheeled past The Brighton Beach Hotel, past the J. Clark Keith Generating Station, and hung a right at the first road leading to the river. Cop cars everywhere. One ambulance, though the ambulance guys were just hanging around having a smoke and finishing their coffee since the guy driving the big black van parked at the edge of the field would be doing all the work after the cops had finished scouring around. The guy with the big black van was Ed the Body Man. He had little cards printed up: *When You're Dead, Call Ed.* Paid to have a sense of humour in his business.

Cec got out of the car and fired off a few shots—Ed's van, the cop cars, the body covered with a sheet. Cec had been around since the advent of the printing press. He knew all the cops by name. He wandered over and talked to the staff sergeant. 'What's up, Harry?'

'Missing person,' said Harry. 'Case solved. She's been found.'

'Can I get in for a closer shot?'

'Wait till the ID guys are done. Then you can shoot away to your heart's content.'

That took a while. I wandered around, talked to the neighbours who were out in their dressing gowns, seeing what was up. Got a couple of quotes I might be able to use. I asked one woman what she thought of it all. She gave me the hard stare. 'The only time *The Star* ever comes down here is when they find a body. Whyn't you come back and do a nice story about us? Before we disappear.'

A visit did seem in order. Like the woman said, the whole community was about to disappear. City council had just decided to buy up all the houses—now you see them, now you don't—tear them down and turn Brighton Beach into an industrial park. Which would be one of your oxymorons.

So.

A few days later I went back. Had a look around.

Brighton Beach was so far down in the west end it was almost out of town. It was so far down the economic scale it didn't register. Lots of little houses here and there. Kind of cottage looking. Some of them neat and clean, nicely painted, well-tended little gardens. Washing on the line. Some a little the worse for wear. Lots of old cars. Some of them without flat tires. Some of the roads paved. Some of them gravel. And look here: A couple of horses nibbling the grass in a fenced yard, right across the road from the body-dumping field.

If you were looking for river people—people who really *lived* the river, had it in their hearts—this would be your first stop. Half the people in the neighbourhood were *born* in the neighbourhood, or had spent most of their lives there.

Time was of the essence.

The first door I knocked on was opened by a fellow named Doug Todd. Fortyish. Friendly. From his front porch you can see three horses, chestnuts, in the corral at the side of the house down at the end of Page, at Water Street, perhaps the only horses in the only corral in the yard of a house anywhere in the city of Windsor. 'At one time, everyone had horses out here. Well, not everyone, but a lot of people. After amalgamation (the city annexed Brighton Beach from Sandwich West Township in the 1960s) when your horse died, you weren't supposed to get another one.' Doug Todd looked at me, then at the horses. 'We could complain. But we don't. I like seeing horses down the street.'

'What brings you down here?' I told him I was interested in finding out about the neighbourhood. 'Coffee?'

Well, sure.

Once upon a time, said Doug, Brighton Beach was a summer place. Cottages down by the river, farm fields further inland. There wasn't much else, except The Brighton Beach Hotel, an old roadhouse with screened-in verandahs and a polished dance floor. It was like a little resort area. People from Detroit used to come over and rent the little cottages along the shore and spend a week fishing and hanging around. All in all, Brighton Beach had been a little corner of heaven, if you couldn't afford a real summer place and you didn't mind the scenery and the smell. Stretch out on a chair in front of one of those long-ago cottages and what you'd be looking at and smelling was Zug Island, directly across the river, less than a mile away—a nightmare of steel mills and foundries. Every so often you'll hear a siren wail and then the stacks begin to spew plumes: Purplish, some of them, yellow, black and white. What billows up out of those stacks and then drifts downwind is anyone's guess. But put it this way: You wouldn't want to lick your finger after dragging it across the hood of your car.

Zug Island is the most aptly named of all the Detroit River islands. It's not really an island—not a natural island anyway. It was created when River Rouge was diverted from its natural course and a U-shaped channel was dredged to allow better shipping access to nearby industries. Zug Island is kind of a picture postcard for all that is wrong with industrialization. Hard to imagine what LaSalle would make of it should he happen back this way four centuries after first sailing past. Probably think he'd landed in hell.

Zug Island is not quite a square mile in size, home of Great Lakes Works, once Detroit Iron Works, now operated by U.S. Steel. The 'Works' was created in 1901, a second blast furnace was built in 1909 and the two—producing pig iron for various foundries—were said to be the largest of their kind in the world. By the 1930s, a third furnace was built, the earlier two were rebuilt and enlarged, and the operations—now a fully integrated steel mill—were a division of the National Steel Corporation. When National Steel went broke in 2003, The Works was purchased by United States Steel, the current operator.

Quite a smell. They say that the Detroit neighbourhoods around Zug Island comprise six of the ten most polluted zip codes in Michigan. You can include the postal code for Brighton Beach as well. Air quality samples contain lead and lots of other nasty stuff, which may account for an inordinate number of cancer and asthma cases in the neighbours who live around Zug Island. Depending on wind direction, the smell can cause you to gag.

I later took a tour of Zug Island and the neighbourhoods around it. Brenda Liveoak, a Detroit environmental activist, was my guide. We couldn't help but notice all the plumes feathering up yellow and white, grey and black, orange and brown over our heads.

'What's in those plumes?'

'Well,' said Brenda, and rhymed them off. Hydrogen sulphide. Carbon monoxide.Carbon dioxide. Naphthalene. Chromium. Benzene. Copper. Lead. Zinc. Iron.

'All those plumes seem to be drifting over to Canada,' I said.

'Yes,' she said. 'The wind's blowing that way.'

'Comforting,' I said.

'Not if you live over there.'

Doug Todd knew all about Zug Island. He grew up looking at it and smelling it. 'I'll show you.' We went out his front door, turned left, walked three blocks down Page, past the horses, crossed Water Street, crossed what was a meadow, and stopped at the water's edge.

'Our place would have been just about here,' he said, tapping his shoe on the dirt embankment.

There had been nine cottages on the riverbank. The one his family rented was dead centre in that row of nine. Plus, there was a house 'built right on the river, on stilts anchored in barrels filled with cement,' which a storm ripped from its footings and sent sailing downriver, a listing seeker of distant shores. 'You can see the barrels. Just over there.'

Doug laughed, looking out at the river. 'My dad had three pigs, him and our neighbour.' His dad and the neighbour would fatten those pigs all winter, eat bacon and ham all spring, summer and fall. 'One of the pigs escaped from its pen. It was out on the river.' He pointed out there. The river was frozen, bluegreen icefloes shelved one atop another. The pig had got out beyond reach and reason, a bewildering distance from shore. 'I can see them yet, father and the neighbour, scrambling and stumbling and cursing, icepan to icepan, floe to floe, to fetch the squealer back to shore.

'That was the end of pigs. They didn't have them after that next spring.'

He laughed. Shook his head.

'Not so bad today.'

'Bad?'

'The smell. Wind's blowing the other way.' From where we stood, quite a vista, smokestacks pluming. Turn around and what we were looking at was a minefield of junk: Tires and roofing shingles, engine blocks and busted toilets, a rusted automobile gasoline tank, aluminum siding and rusted-out mufflers, dryers and freezers, love seats and tub chairs, three-legged tables and two-legged chairs, a cracked motorcycle helmet and a rusted bedspring, the white plastic spinner from a washing machine, a child's big-wheel with a rear wheel missing, three garbage bags and the contents of an ashtray.

'Drives us crazy,' said Doug. 'People from the city just come out and dump their junk right here.' He shook his head.

'And bodies,' I said.

'And bodies,' he said.

'What was it like, living by the river?'

'It was neat. First thing every morning you're sitting on the dock seeing what's going on.' What was going on, mostly, was Great Lakes Steel fuming and pluming across the river, and freighters and ferries churning upstream and down. Doug remembered the names of a couple: *The Cleveland Cliffs*, a freighter, and the *Aquarama,* a cruise ship.'You'd see them coming, you'd wade out to your waist or your armpits and wait for the wake to wash you back in. The beach is mostly pebbles, but there are sandy patches. Two or four feet out from shore it gets sandy. You'd jump in the water as a kid, practically every morning from early May to the end of October. Best place in the world to live, as a kid.'

He pointed down the shore. 'Nine cottages in all and there were three or four boat liveries run from those nine cottages.' At the far upstream end of the string of cottages there was a livery run by Dal Chase and his wife. 'Theirs was the biggest, I'd say. They had 60 or 70 steel boats. Dan and his wife lived in a trailer.' In the middle of the row, next to the cottage where Doug and his family lived, were the Beaumonts. 'Uncle Chuck Beaumont ran a livery, too. He had nine kids. Eight or nine. Everyone had big families then. The liveries kept us kids busy, carrying tackle from boats to cars for an American quarter.' Most of the customers were Americans, almost all of them black. 'And a quarter was a lot of money.' The quarters went on black balls, five for a nickel, from the jar on the counter at Mrs. Hawchuk's store. Instant fingerprints.

'We got our water from a well. One well for everyone.

'All the places had outhouses out back.

'If you were sitting in the outhouse at night with the door open you could see the freighters going past in the space between the cottages; if you looked above the roof of your cottage you could see the lights on the stacks of the steel plants across the river. Which was odd, eh? We didn't have electricity. We didn't get it until 1952 or '53. We used oil lamps.'

It was the next year, 1954 or 1955, he thinks, that his family was told to go.

'We could take our houses with us, but we had to go.'

So they moved inland.

'What keeps you here?'

'My father, my brother and sister are all within walking distance.'

His father's backyard backs onto his brother's backyard. His sister lives three doors down. Now, the sister's daughter has just moved into a house in the neighbourhood. 'So there's another generation.'

'You should go see my dad. He'd tell you a story or two.'

'Where's his place?'

'Go up Page to Sandwich, hang a right, then a left on Broadway. You can't miss it. It's a one-storey white-sided bungalow on the left.

'He drives a blue pickup with a tailgate lift. If it's in the drive, he's home. If it's not, he's not.'

We walked back to his place. 'Another one you should definitely talk to is Tom Reaume. His dad owned The Brighton Beach Hotel. He's got a story or two.'

I wrote the name in my notebook.

One last question: 'What will I miss? Not being able to walk to the river. Not being able to do things I've done all my life. Not being able to take my grandson for a walk by the river where I went when I was a kid. Things like that.'

*　　　*　　　*

THERE ARE LOTS OF REASONS TO VISIT DETROIT, OF COURSE.

Some people go for the shopping. My wife remembers the days when her parents would load the five kids into the station wagon and head over to Detroit where they'd spend the day shopping in one of the downtown department stores—Crowley's, J.L. Hudson's. Then they'd cut off all the price tags, throw away their old clothes and put on three or four shirts and a couple of pairs of pants each and head back to the border looking like Pillsbury dough boys and girls.

'Anything to declare?'

'No. Not a thing.'

People still go shopping, but now it's to suburban malls.

People go for the theatre and the opera and the ballet. They go to The Detroit Institute of Arts, one of America's really fine museums, at least until the now bankrupt city sells the art.

People go over to eat: Greektown or Mexican Town are still favoured spots; and, of course, they go over to watch Lions and Wings games.

But, for us, Detroit has always been synonymous with the Tigers.

And the Tigers were always synonymous with Tiger Stadium.

Loved that place.

It was located at the corner of Michigan and Trumbull in Detroit's old Corktown area. And for more than a century 'The Corner' was a huge part of the life of the city.

There's no place on earth quite like an old ballpark. And there was definitely no place like Tiger Stadium. Okay, maybe Fenway and Wrigley and the original Yankee Stadium. That's about it.

It was built on the site of Bennett Park, the Tigers' first home. The old park, completed in 1895, had wooden grandstands, and in some areas the edge of the outfield was marked off by a rope looped between wooden posts.

Frank Navin bought the Tigers in 1911. His next order of business was replacing Bennett Park with a 23,000-seat stadium. Navin Field opened April 20, 1912, the same day Boston's Fenway Park swung open its gates.

Over the years the stadium was expanded and renamed. It became Briggs Stadium after Walter Briggs bought the team. Eventually the Tigers had an owner, John Fetzer, who didn't want to name the park after himself—or name it after a big-time corporate sponsor. Fetzer named it, simply, Tiger Stadium. How perfect is that? And how perfect was that old ballpark? It was named a State of Michigan Historic Site in 1975 and was on the National Register of Historic Places since 1989. And still they tore it down.

Makes you wonder: If they've still got Fenway Park and Wrigley Field with all their quirks and charms, why on earth don't we still have a Tiger Stadium? Nice as Comerica Park is, it doesn't hold a candle to Tiger Stadium. You're so far away from the action in the upper deck of the new ballpark that you need binoculars to see the players. Which was surely *not* the case in the old ballpark. And since when did you need a merry-go-round in a ballpark?

We didn't need a merry-go-round. We needed a ball game. Period. But first, after parking the car in one of the $5 Corktown lots, we needed a beer, and for that we'd make our way to Hoot Robinson's bar on Trumbull, just down from the Checker Cab building. Mandatory stop an hour or so before game time. The place was long and narrow. Bar on one side, kitchen at the back. Beers cases stacked from the floor halfway to the ceiling. The beer was always cold, the dogs and burgers were always good, and the men's john featured a trough urinal—must've been about twelve, fifteen feet long—which Hoot filled with buckets of ice.

Hoot was the old guy behind the bar: White hair (what was left of it), thin, energetic, and always quick with a quip.

Once upon a time, when the world was a little different than it is today, baseball players would come into Hoot's and ask for a beer and a hotdog *before* the game. Some of them did not restrict themselves to *a* beer or *a* hotdog. Babe Ruth, for instance, could scarf down half-a-dozen dogs and three or four beers *and then* cross the street and hammer a hanging curve ball over the right-field roof onto Trumbull, bouncing it off the front wall of Hoot's place.

'You're shittin' us, right Hoot?'

'I shit you not, boys.'

You're shitting us, right?

I'm offended you would suggest such a thing, he said.

Come on. Babe Ruth going into some downtown dive right before a game?

First, Hoot's was not a dive. And second, times have changed.

They haven't changed that much, she said.

Once upon a time ...

No way.

In fact, yes. Not only that ....

ONCE UPON A TIME, THE DETROIT LIONS USED TO PLAY AT TIGER STADIUM. When I first arrived in town, Bill Shields, then *The Star*'s City Hall reporter, and his wife Gloria took me to a game. But before going inside Tiger Stadium, we cut across Trumbull and edged our way through the throngs until we were within shouting distance of Hoot. 'Six beers, six dogs.' 'What kind of beer?' 'Anything cold.' Half an hour later, we headed back across Trumbull and through the gates and up the ramp to our seats. Froze our arses off, but what a great after-noon. Can't remember who the Lions were playing, can't remember who won or lost. But I remember the noise, the laughter, fans razzing each other, fans filling their coffee cups from flasks fished from coat pockets. Just what a football afternoon should be.

So, as you might expect, if Babe Ruth could zip in for a quick one or three, why wouldn't the football players?

'Bobby Layne used to come in.'

'Bobby Layne?'

'The Lions quarterback. Put the Lions on his shoulder and took them to the NFL Championships. Back in the '50s.'

'Now you are shittin' us, Hoot.'

'Cross my heart,' said Hoot. 'He sat right there, third stool from the end.'

'And the Babe?'

'Always stood. End of the bar. Right there.'

'Go on.'

'You can ask anyone. Any of the old regulars. They'll tell you.'

'They're all dead.'

'Well, I'm not. And I'm tellin' you. The Babe, he stood right there, big as life and twice as noisy. And Bobby? He sat right there. Hardly sayin' a word. Just havin' a quiet beer and a couple of dogs before heading off to work. Just like the guys on the line.'

So that was Hoot Robinson's bar.

How much better can game-day get?

There was something magical about walking into Tiger Stadium. It was always a little dank and it smelled of stale beer and mustard, with maybe a touch of mould. But go in through the gates and up the walk-ways to the upper deck and the place would stop you in your tracks. That green green field with the infield dirt raked and groomed and watered and the chalk lines as perfect and straight and white as they could be. Better than W.P. Kinsella's *Field of Dreams*.

Took your breath away.

Does even now, just thinking about it.

We preferred the upper deck—usually left field, sometimes right. The view was awesome. In Tiger Stadium, the upper deck extended out over the lower deck so that if you got front-row seats—and back then front-row seats were easy to come by—you were directly above the front-row seats in the lower deck. Lean over the rail and there's the left fielder. You could call down to him. Sometimes he'd turn and wave. The year I'm thinking of, 1995, it was Bobby Higginson. Twenty-four years old, first year in the majors, more hustle than a Las Vegas card shark. He was five years away from his best year—30 home runs, 102 runs driven in, a .300 batting average—but you could tell by looking at him that there were big things in his future. Maybe he was just what the Tigers needed. They needed something: They were headed for a 60-84 strike-shortened season. Hurts to write it.

Some days just stay with you. And this day I'm thinking of—a perfect Sunday afternoon in May—my son Adam and I were up in left field. Sunday, May 28, 1995. We had front-row seats, upper-deck left field. Section 5, Row 1, seats 3 and 4.

Fifth inning, Tigers were up 10-9.

But top of the sixth, guess who was coming up to bat?

They didn't call him The Big Hurt for nothing. Before the year was out, he'd be waving to the fans at the All-Star Game, and then go on to finish with 40 homers, 111 runs driven in and a .308 batting average.

So you tell me why, with Frank Thomas about to come to bat, the guys next to us—in seats 5 and 6—would excuse themselves and squeeze past us and head out for a hot dog and a beer.

A few minutes later, they were standing in line watching the television screen above the concession-booth window, waiting to place their order. So they had an excellent view, and could see the replay as well, as Adam shuffled a couple of steps to his left—just about exactly between seats 5 and 6—and made a perfect highlight reel two-handed catch of Frank Thomas' line-drive homer which tied the game at 10.

Ten or fifteen minutes later the beer-and-dog boys returned. 'Was that you?' said the one guy, 'Who caught the home-run ball?'

Adam held up the ball.

'And you were standing in front of our seats?'

Adam shrugged and smiled.

'Sonofabitch,' said the one.

'Talk about perfect timing,' said his buddy.

The Tigers?

Lost 14-12.

But we were getting used to that.

SEEMS TO ME THEY USED TO HAVE A LOT MORE MID-WEEK AFTERNOON GAMES in those days, but it could just be memory playing tricks. Anyway, one mid-week afternoon there I was—upper deck, right field this time—and I kid you not, I was the only person in the entire section. Okay. The usher makes two.

I smiled at him. He nodded. I headed up to the very back row. Got settled in. Opened a new page in my scorebook, started working on the line-ups. And once the game got going, I fired up a lovely Cuban I'd brought with me, a nice all-day Cohiba. Beer, baseball, Cohiba. Perfect. Does life get any better than this? Ever?

A couple of innings in, I was looking for the beer kid. Then I thought, what beer kid would come all the way up to upper deck right field when there's only one guy there?

Well, I still had the cigar.

I noticed the usher looking at me every now and then. Every time I noticed, I smiled and nodded. He did the same.

Three innings in, he started the slow ascent to my back-row perch.

'Sir?'

'Yes.'

'I'm afraid I have to inform you that this here's a no-smoking section.'

I looked at him. Then I looked to my right. Then I looked to my left. Apart from me and the usher, still no one else around.

I smiled at the usher. 'I have the feeling someone just told you to come and tell me this.'

'Yes sir.'

'And we're on someone's camera, I take it.'

'Yes sir.'

'Very good. So whoever is watching us on camera now knows you've done your job. And if anyone asks, I'd be happy to tell them you did your job. Very politely, I must say.'

'Thank you, sir.'

'How about this? Should any of these people to my left'—I scanned the seats to my left— 'or any of these people to my right'—I scanned the equally empty seats to my right—'complain about my cigar, I'll be quite happy to put it out right away.'

'Very good, sir. I believe this is all taken care of.'

'Thank you,' I said.

'And thank you, sir.'

Down he went, resumed his patrol of the aisle which paralleled the field. And I resumed my game-watching and score-keeping and cigar smoking.

And everyone lived happily ever after.

Try that, these days.

OKAY, ONE MORE.

Every couple of weeks, whenever the Tigers were home and there was a mid-week afternoon game, I'd get a call.

'Hi. It's Don.'

'What time?'

'Say 11:30. Twelve?'

'See you there.'

End of conversation. Don was Don Gonyea, then working for public radio in Detroit (and later NPR's White House correspondent) and one of the most ardent Tigers' fans I've ever met. 'See you there' meant, of course, Hoot Robinson's Bar.

This particular afternoon a couple of my Windsor buddies—Dave and Nes—came along and we all wound up in upper deck right field. It was one of those perfect summer days: 80 degrees or so, a cooling breeze, more beer boys than you could shake a bat at, and great seats, three rows up from the rail. I forget the inning, but pretty early on we were all watching the game, telling stories and jokes, and suddenly Dave recoiled. 'Oh shit.'

And sure enough, he had a great gob of pigeon poo just to the right of centre, dripping nicely down along his temple toward his cheek. Once we stopped laughing, which took a minute or two, we gave him all the napkins we could muster, and off he went to the washroom.

Ten or fifteen minutes later he returned, hair cleaned and slicked down, no visible signs of pigeon shit anywhere. Nes wondered if he should give Dave the sniff test, or whether we should let him rejoin us regardless. 'You *could* buy me a beer,' said Dave. The least we could do.

The beer boy arrived, as if on cue: 'Four of your finest.'

'You got any extra paper napkins?'

We settled back in. And I'm not kidding you, Dave hadn't had more than three sips of beer before—'oh, SHIT'—he dropped his beer, jumped up, looked up, looked down, and sure enough another great gob of pigeon shit had landed in just about the same place. We gave him the napkins the beer kid had given us. Off he went.

When he came back there was no one in our seats.

'Up here,' said Don.

Dave looked up. There we were, as far up as we could get (just about where I'd had my Cohiba that day). Nes pointed up to the rafters. No pigeons.

'You're safe.'

*   *   *

I RAN INTO ANTHONY QUILLER AT THE KRESGE'S COUNTER——GRILLED CHEESE and a glass of milk, 35 cents. We chatted for a minute or two about a case he'd been working. A woman accused of stabbing her husband while he slept. I told him I'd been following the trial.

'She guilty?'

'I can't comment on that,' he said, 'since I'm defending her.'

'Of course,' I said.

'But let's just say if she were guilty—hypothetically speaking, of course—he had it coming.'

I swallowed, had another bite, swallowed again. 'Oh?' I said.

He smiled. Seems the phone rang. Husband was downstairs. Wife was upstairs. Unbeknownst to him, his wife picked up at precisely the moment he did and he didn't realize it. 'It was the girlfriend.'

'Not too swift, her calling him at home.'

'No,' said Quiller. 'Not too swift. Neither was he. They started chatting about their last romantic encounter, and then arranged the next one. Smoochy, smoochy. See you tomorrow. Same place? Same place. A convenient parking spot down past the bridge. And they hung up. Middle of the night he woke up with a knife right where it hurts the most. Blood all over the bed.'

'Parts missing?'

'Just about.'

I smiled.

He smiled.

I finished my sandwich. He was working on his coffee. 'Speaking of knives,' he said. 'You ever hear about the Slasher?'

'The Slasher.' He had my attention.

'Remind me to tell you about him,' he said. He dropped a tip on the counter and headed for the door.

*　　　*　　　*

This Quiller fellow, she said.

Yes? he said.

I've looked through the Law Society's records. There's no record of him at all.

Errors and omissions, he said.

What's that mean?

Not all records are complete.

Did he exist?

Exist? he said.

Was he a real person? she said.

Very real, he said.

You sure?

Very sure, he said.

The Slasher?

He was real as well. Very real.

*　　　*　　　*

WINDSOR WAS DEFINITELY A DIFFERENT TOWN BACK IN THE 1940S. Very gritty, especially the waterfront. All those bars and bordellos. Very appealing to a certain clientele. Very appalling to the solid citizens who saw what went on there as nothing less than 'evil'. Fodder for those Sunday sermons.

The Slasher's name was Ronald Sears. Caused quite the stir in 1945-46. Windsor hardly ever had any murders. Then, over a two week period in the summer of 1945, three men were killed, and a fourth was taken to hospital with near-fatal wounds.

The murders were gruesome. Two of the victims had been stabbed repeatedly in the chest and back, and one of them had been slashed brutally in the buttocks as well. The head of the third victim had been crushed with a hammer. *The Star* obliged with lurid crime-scene photos. There were stories about a precipitous rise in the rate of sex crimes.

As if people weren't sufficiently freaked out, one of the cops said they were clearly dealing with 'a sadist of the worst type, a maniac.' Shades of Jack-the-Ripper.

The Star couldn't resist. It ran an editorial under the headline 'This Fiend Must Be Caught,' describing the Slasher as a monster of 'senseless blood-lust... with a perverted mind.'

It seemed obvious to *The Star*, the preachers, and the cops that the likely suspect would be found among the riff-raff congregating down in the very dodgy bars and whorehouses by the river. The cops rounded up more than a hundred homeless men. A month later, all the homeless were back on the streets. No arrests.

A year after the three killings, two more men were similarly attacked.

They survived, and talked. Admitted to the cops they'd gone down to the river looking for other gay men. They'd found a willing partner, but just as things were getting interesting, the partner pulled out a knife.

'The attacks took place right about here.' Anthony Quiller and I were standing on Riverside Drive, foot of Crawford Avenue. This was about a week after he'd first told me about the Slasher, and a few minutes after we'd finished another lunch at the Kresge's counter.

'Back then, all this area,' he pointed down toward the river and the railway lines, 'this was a vacant field. It was kind of a haunt for homosexuals.'

'How'd they catch him?'

'Luckily for the cops, Sears left a knife in one of his victims. The cops released a photo of the knife, *The Star* printed the picture and mentioned that there was a $3,000 reward for information leading to the killer's arrest.'

'Big money.'

'Was at the time. And Sears' sister-in-law collected it. She identi-fied the knife as part of Sears' collection of knives, and the cops went around to the house and picked him up.' He was just a kid —eighteen years old. He was charged with the murder of Hugh Blackwood-Price, a war veteran who was wearing his Essex Scottish uniform when he was killed in August 1945.

'When Sears was asked in court why he had stabbed Hugh Black-wood-Price, he testified that he'd been sexually assaulted by a man when he was nine years old. He said he thought the victim was a per-vert, and so he stabbed him.'

'What happened to him?'

'He was sentenced to hang,' said Quiller. 'But an appeal court ruled that the only evidence against Sears was his own confession, and that Sears had only confessed because the cops grilled him for seven hours, non-stop. They'd forgotten to mention he could have a lawyer present if he wished.

'Missed a date with the hangman by three weeks.'

'Then what?'

'He was convicted of attempted murder. Sentenced to 12 years in prison. They sent him to Kingston, but a psychiatrist said he was schizophrenic. They sent him to the Mental.'

'And?'

'He died there. Caught TB in 1956.'

*   *   *

ELEVEN TRIPS PAST HIS HOUSE AND A WEEK LATER, THERE WAS ANDY TODD'S pickup: Angled in by the garage behind the house, back wheels on the lawn, front wheels on the drive.

Andy's garage was three cars wide. There was a double door on the right and a window to the left of it and between the door and the window a hand-lettered sign: NO SCRAPE.

There was a light on in the garage, and through the window I could see a man standing in the side doorway, adjusting his pants. I waited until he was finished adjusting.

'Andy Todd?'

Andy Todd looked at me the way he might look at a city by-laws officer. Or a cop. Or a politician.

I introduced myself. Told him I'd spent an interesting hour or so with his son Doug, talking about growing up in the little place by the river.

'They were just old shacks down by the river,' Andy said. 'No foundations. No plumbing, no wiring, no frills. No hassles. One bedroom, kitchen, living room. Pretty small.'

Crowded?

'Crowded? Oh yeah. Don't tell me, baby. Yes sir.'

But the price was right: Three dollars a month paid, as Andy recalled, to the Great Lakes Copper Mine Company Limited of New York City. This was 1948 or so.

That little three-dollar-a-month shack was 'A-okay with me. I couldn't care less what it looked like.' What he did care about was that he could drag his wrecks home and park them in the yard. 'Buy a car, wreck it, sell it. Parts or scrap. Scrap mostly.

'Nobody bothered me.'

Not like they would have if he'd lived in the city.

'I don't like the city. I like, what do you call it? Freedom. Freedom. I like that.'

The freedom lasted until 1953 or 1954, when the company told him to move, with his shack or without. He moved. Without.

First, he moved to a place on Matchette Road, then to this place, which he built in 1955, just about the time 'my ex buggered off and left me with the kids, alone. Six, counting Vincent.' And he names them, in order: 'Dolores, Richard, Sandra, Douglas, Vincent and Donna.'

And here in that hand-built, one-storey, white-sided house on Broadway Street, he's stayed ever since.

Behind him in the garage: Half-a-dozen barrels filled with pipe and wiring and bits of metal; the bed of a pickup truck, filled with more junk, sitting on the floor. All of it for sale, for a price.

'I didn't go to school. I work so hard. I had to. A big family. Six kids. If it wouldn't have been for garbage, I'd never have been able to carry on.'

Garbage, rooting through it, taking what's valuable—aluminum, copper, steel, plastic, furniture, appliances—hauling it home, sorting it, stacking and storing it, selling it or bartering with it, has been Andy Todd's trade for more than 60 years.

It was garbage which sustained him when he landed in Canada in 1929—unhappy timing—from his native Macedonia. It was garbage which sustained him when he was making 35 cents a day working as a general labourer for Sandwich West Township. Garbage augmented his income when he worked for Huron Steel until his retirement, without company pension, at age 70. Garbage which sustained him the 14 years since.

'It's the only way I can survive. I get $680 a month Canada pension. Old age pension. You can't continue on $680 a month. Taxes, heat, light.'

So, most days, Andy Todd was up by 5 AM. By six he was wheeling his pickup into alleyways, picking up for nothing the things which the affluent tossed into the garbage, the things which ended up in one barrel or another, in the garage behind his house, things he could sell.

'I work my ass off.

'A lot of people my age, they're half-dead.

'Or all dead.

'Me?

'I work like a slave.'

I asked him if he ever considered moving, given that the city was buying people out, to make way for an industrial park.

'They're not going to move me out of here. I can tell you that.

'I'm gonna die here.

'Yessirree.'

The reason for Andy Todd's resolve?

Andy Todd married in 1941.

By the time he and his wife moved to Brighton Beach seven years later, they had five children, plus the daughter his wife had brought to the marriage. 'She just buggered off. Left me with the kids, alone.

'One got killed. Early one morning. Right out front.

'He was getting ready to go to school. And this goddamned guy, he's looking at the field and he's driving along. I seen him. There's enough room for three cars on that road but he's looking at the field instead of where he was going.

'I seen him.

'I saw him go right over the boy.

'I saw it.

'I can see it now.

'Every goddamned second of it.'

I asked Andy how old his boy was.

'Nine.'

I asked his name.

'Vincent.'

Half an hour of questions about his business, his home, his neighbourhood, Andy fired off a question of his own: 'Why are you asking me all these questions?'

I told him I was operating on the same principle as he: I was going around collecting bits and pieces of a story. 'When my barrel's full I'll tip it over and see what I've got.'

He smiled, nodded.

'That's the way to do it.'

*   *   *

SOME THINGS ARE JUST TOO GOOD TO LAST.

We were sitting down by the river, this would have been a month or two after Ethel came back from Africa. Late August, late in the day. The sun was setting over Windsor. We were *definitely* not in Windsor. We, as Ethel had pointed out early on, were in Riverside. (One day she said to me: 'I'm going in to Windsor today. Can I get you anything?') It had become our custom to have cocktails on the patio once I got home from work, showered and changed. It was always peaceful down there. Though you could hear the traffic on Riverside Drive, it was a distant sound, like we were in another world. Mostly what you could hear was the wind and the birds in the trees.

'I'm terribly sorry,' she said. 'I have some unpleasant news.'

I thought for a moment she had received some bad news from the doctor.

As it turned out, it was bad news for me.

'I'm putting the place up for sale.'

Seven words. Knife in the heart.

'I'm buying an apartment.' By which she meant condominium— something relatively new in Windsor. They'd built a big new one just down the road—in Windsor, of all places—and she'd signed up for a penthouse. 'It will be for the best, I expect. It's quite spacious, with a wonderful view. I'd like you to see it.'

'Quite spacious' didn't do it credit. Three bedrooms, library, living room, dining room, three baths and a balcony that extended the full width of her living room and half the width of the building itself, wrapping around one corner of the building. It afforded a commanding view of Belle Isle and, further west, the skyline of Detroit.

'It'll be perfect,' she said, 'what with all my travelling.'

Perfect, except given all the security personnel there'd be no need for a houseboy.

'I hope you'll understand.'

'Yes,' I said. 'Of course.'

'It'll be a couple of months before the decorators are done.'

So. Two months notice.

I savoured all the moments I could.

*   *   *

MY NEXT ENCOUNTER WITH MRS. MAJOR WAS A KIND OF FIELD TRIP. She thought since I'd done such a bang-up job on Colonel Prince, I should do a piece on the War of 1812.

'Which happened right here,' she said, tapping her toe on the sidewalk of Pitt Street. 'This house,' she said, 'was central to the goings on.' Wasn't much of a house. Two storeys back of the Cleary Auditorium.

'Ah,' she said, when I'd said as much. 'Appearances can be deceiving.'

And thus began a half-hour's lecture on the importance of the François Baby House, which is what we were standing there staring at. What we were staring at was not exactly the François Baby House. Not the original, anyway. 'The original house faced the other way, for one thing,' said Mrs. Major. 'And the property extended all the way to the river.'

'How'd it get turned around?'

'It was rebuilt. Don't ask me how they could have got it that wrong. But they did.'

So here it was, rebuilt backwards on a tiny portion of the original lot, the remainder now being occupied by buildings facing Riverside Drive and Dieppe Gardens down by the river.

François Baby was a magistrate, a member of the Legislative Assembly of Upper Canada, and a local bigwig. Work crews began building the house in the spring of 1812. Bad timing. Before the house was even finished the American general William Hull, in charge of Fort Detroit, invaded Canada and took over Baby's mansion as his headquarters. Major General Isaac Brock chased him back across the river, and then he moved into Baby's house and used it as his headquarters. 'So you see,' said Mrs. Major, 'this property was instrumental in the surrender of Detroit.'

Actually, I didn't see that at all, and mentioned as much.

'Well,' said Mrs. Major.

And here's the story, much abbreviated and without Mrs. Major's hand-clutching for emphasis:

When Brock heard that Hull had crossed the river and invaded Canada, he called for volunteers and made his way to Amherstburg. They arrived—about 300 strong—on the 13th of August. That night, Brock met Chief Tecumseh, and they came up with a plan to attack Fort Detroit.

Hull, learning that they were coming, hightailed it back to Detroit. Brock installed a couple of gun batteries on François Baby's property. On the 15th of August, 1812, he sent a message to Hull, demanding his surrender. Hull said he'd do no such thing. Brock fired a few volleys across the river. The Americans fired a few right back. Then they all went to bed.

Early next morning, General Brock, his soldiers, his militia, and his Indian allies under the command of Chief Tecumseh, made their way across the river about three miles below Fort Detroit, then marched along the river and lined up in front of the fort. Brock was hoping the Americans would come out and fight. 'Much to his surprise,' said Mrs. Major, 'Hull surrendered.'

Well, perhaps not such a surprise after all. I later saw a copy of the letter which Brock had sent to Hull. I'll highlight the significant sentence:

'The force at my disposal authorizes me to require of you the immediate surrender of Fort Detroit. *It is far from my intention to join in a war of extermination, but you must be aware that the numerous body of Indians who have attached themselves to my troops will be beyond control the moment the contest commences.* You will find me disposed to enter into such conditions as will satisfy the most scrupulous sense of honour. Lieutenant-Colonel McDonnell and Major Glegg are fully authorized to conclude any arrangement that may lead to prevent the unnecessary effusion of blood.'

The bit about extermination and out-of-control Indians did the trick.

The white flag went up. And at 12 o'clock, Brock found himself in charge of Fort Detroit, which was conveniently full of guns and ammunition.

As is often the case when it comes to war, all of this didn't really matter one way or another. The following year, Detroit was recaptured by U.S. General William Henry Harrison (who would go on to become president). And in 1814, General Hull was court-martialed for cowardice and sentenced to die. President James Madison, however, remitted the sentence.

And François Baby got his house back.

'So you see,' said Mrs. Major.

'Yes,' I said. 'I see.'

*　　　*　　　*

AS FOR ME, IT WAS FAREWELL TO RIVERFRONT LIVING AND BACK TO THE ATTIC. I found a place up on Ouellette Avenue, right across from the emergency entrance to Hotel Dieu Hospital. Two-and-a-half-storeys, red brick, owned by Anna Grayson and her husband Tony.

Anna—who died as I was writing this—was a violinist with the Windsor Symphony back in the days of Matti Holli. Her husband Tony, dutiful husband that he was, went to the symphony to hear Anna and the rest of the gang, but regularly fell asleep. 'I find it very restful,' he told me once. Quite the smile. When he wasn't snoozing at the Symphony, Tony fixed watches in a second-floor cubbyhole above the family's jewellery store down on Ouellette near the river. The house on Ouellette had quite a pedigree. Before the Graysons bought it, Frances Baby Davis lived there, descended from François Baby—the *Baby House* Baby—widow of the former mayor John Davis.

My room was up there in the half-storey at the top. A little on the small side, sloping ceilings and a smallish window giving onto Ouellette. Spring through fall, you had to keep the window cranked open to avoid suffocating. Wonderful when the ambulances came screaming in at two in the morning. Apart from that, a pretty nice place. The noise—ambulances and constant street traffic—made for a nice ambience in my second novel, which was set in that attic room.

Want to have a look at the place, you should hurry along.

A doctor bought the place and is going to tear it down to make room for a parking lot for his clinic, in the house adjacent.

If Mrs. Major had still been around, she'd have been apoplectic. The Graysons' place was one of eight lovely old houses (well, most of them lovely) which line the block, at the northern corner of which is The Medical Arts building, just nicely restored. On the main street. She would have seen it as an outrage. She would have gone to city council to scold them about destroying one of the last significant streetscapes on Ouellette. 'On *The Main Street*,' she would have said. Eyebrows arched.

She would have been ignored, of course.

You know what Joni Mitchell said about parking lots.

WE HAVE A HABIT OF TEARING DOWN OLD BUILDINGS IN WINDSOR. Much to Mrs. Major's, and others', dismay. The most grievous recent example was when city council gave the nod to the expropriation and demolition of the entire block of turn-of-the-century storefronts— including Lee's and South Shore Books, the city's best little independent bookstore, not to mention The Press Club and The Paradise,

Gino's Italian Village, Varsity Sports, a neat little tea room, the name of which escapes me—to make way for a nasty bit of modern expediency: An office tower and parking garage. For those of us around at the time when the Norwich Block came down, it's hard to walk by the place without a little shiver of sorrow.

On the other hand, there are few who still decry the loss of buildings on the other side of Riverside Drive. And there used to be lots of them. When I came to town, the riverfront wasn't much to look at. There was a little park at the foot of Ouellette, and as for the rest, if you liked rail lines, rail sheds, roundhouses, warehouses, whorehouses and factories, you were in luck.

Great Western Railway built the first lines along the waterfront in 1854. By the time I got to town a century later, the rail lines were six or eight abreast from Riverside Drive to the river's edge, extending from Hiram Walker's to the foot of Caron Avenue. The old CN station was on the river-side of Riverside, at the foot of Goyeau Street. The CPR station—complete with its signature turret roof—was near the foot of Caron Avenue. There was a Michigan Central station between Elm and Cameron. There were rail sheds and an old turntable to turn the trains around so they could go back whence they came. There were docks for the ferries which carried the train cars back and forth across the river. In other words: A working riverfront.

As for parks, there was Dieppe Gardens, named in memory of the soldiers of the Essex-Kent Scottish Regiment killed during the World War II landing at Dieppe, France in 1942. The property was once a docking site for the Detroit-Windsor Ferry Company. There were some old cottages, a couple of retail stores and hotels, and at one time, *The Border Cities Star* building down at the foot of Riverside and Ferry Street. But in the late '50s, the city bought the property, knocked down the buildings, and created the park. Hard to imagine, back then, that the rest of the riverfront would one day look the same—all grass, and gardens, trees, walkways and park benches.

From Dieppe Gardens to the bridge: Old warehouses and empty fields, lots of weeds.

One of the last buildings on the north side of the drive was the British American Hotel, known simply as the B.A. to one and all. It stood at the foot of Ouellette and extended from Riverside almost all the way down to the river. Very popular spot. And it was very nearly replaced with a towering modern hotel. Back in the '70s, a hotel chain from Kitchener-Waterloo wanted to knock down the B.A. and build a high-rise hotel to be called the Valhalla Inn. The mayor at the time, Frank Wansbrough—Wansy, to just about everyone in town, a man who apparently was born with a cigar stuck in his mouth—liked the idea, and called his aldermen to a closed-door meeting to discuss it. He later said that everyone, with one exception, said 'go for it'. The one holdout thought the idea needed to be studied more carefully. That holdout was Bert Weeks.

Bert was a man accustomed to rowing against the tide. There were lots of people in town—not just on council—who saw nothing wrong in having buildings on the waterfront. Parks were nice, but parks didn't pay taxes. Bert didn't see it that way. He didn't think there should be any commercial development on the waterfront. His dream was to have a park from the bridge in the west all the way to the Hiram Walker complex in the east.

He was so confident of that vision that he ran against Wansy and the main plank of his campaign was that there would be no development on the river. He said if someone wanted to build a hotel, there was lots of room on the other side of the street. Big surprise for Wansy. He went to bed election night in 1975 confident he'd won a squeaker, and woke up the next morning to discover Bert the new mayor. That was it for the Valhalla proposal, and that was the turning point for our riverfront. Bit by bit, as land became available, the city snapped it up, tore out the rail lines, knocked down the buildings, planted grass and flowers, installed walking paths and bike paths, and managed, just as Bert had dreamed, to create a waterfront that is the envy of many larger cities (Toronto with its maze of waterfront condos comes to mind).

One visionary tends to spawn others.

Lou Odette grew up in Windsor and made his fortune here with the family-owned Eastern Construction company. Though he later moved to Toronto, his hometown was never far from mind. The family has a long history of philanthropic endeavours here (the Odette School of Business at The University of Windsor is just one), but none is more public than the sculpture garden which was his brainchild. In 1981, he donated the pieces of outdoor sculpture (there are now more than 30) that are placed along the river.

You can't miss them: From life-sized elephants and penguins to whimsical mermaids and dancing bears, men on horseback and Eve's apple. They're placed all along the riverfront from the foot of the bridge to the foot of Church Street, across from The Art Gallery of Windsor.

Just perfect: An outdoor art gallery open all year round free of charge, which is a blessing and a surprise for tourists and home-town folks alike.

Tip of the cap to the Odette family and to the visionaries in Windsor who said: 'Sculptures? On the riverfront? Why not?'

*   *   *

SUMMER NIGHTS IN THE NEWSROOM. ONCE WE WERE FINISHED OUR assignments, we'd take a break, go over to the windows on the Pitt Street side of the building, pull up some chairs, open the windows, light up and watch the river. Every now and then a freighter would slip past, upbound or down. Always got you thinking.

'Wonder what that would be like.'

'What what would be like?' said Larry. Larry was thin as a broom. Black hair slicked back Elvis-style. He'd parked his bucket in the corner, mop stuck in the water, handle leaning against the wall. He was sitting beside me, feet up on the radiator, having a smoke.

'Working on a freighter.'

'Different,' he said.

'It'd be kind of fun. Always on the go.'

'As long as you didn't get seasick.'

When I was a kid, I'd go down to the harbour in Owen Sound and look at the freighters. There were always two or three tied up at a time. They'd come in to load up at the grain elevators. They weren't very big—three or four hundred feet—the ones that went to the smaller harbours around the Great Lakes. But they looked pretty big to me. I sometimes thought it would be a good way to spend your life. Going from Toronto to Cleveland, Detroit to Chicago, up to the Sault, over to Fort William. All of which I mentioned to Larry.

'You'd probably be bored witless.'

'There'd always be something interesting to see in those places. Chicago, all the bars, all that music.'

'I dunno. I think I'd go squirrely cooped up on a boat. You'd be with the same guys months on end. How many poker games could you take with the same four guys?'

'You could read. Lots of time to read and think.'

'Not too great for your love life,' said Larry. 'Unless you were into sailors. Or unless you had a girl in every port. I bet most of those guys aren't married. How could you be married and be out on the lakes eight, nine months a year?'

'Might be a good way to save a marriage. You wouldn't get on each other's nerves. You'd come home and she'd be happy to see you.'

'Unless she was being happy with someone else while you were gone.'

'Yeah. There's that.'

'I heard a story about that,' I said. 'This guy, let's call him Lenny, was a deckhand on the lake boats. Got home once a month or so, whenever his boat tied up in Owen Sound. His wife was carrying on something fierce while he was away. He kind of suspected, just by a few things she said. Then someone wrote him—his brother or someone—and told him what was going on.

'His wife, she was always reading the shipping news so she knew when his boat was coming in, and she'd make sure to give the place the once-over, no revealing telltale signs, no strange shoes under the bed, that sort of thing.

'But didn't he fool her? Told his captain there was a family emergency he had to deal with, got off the boat in Collingwood and took the bus over from there. Waited until evening, then walked up to his place. Strange pickup in the drive. Let himself in, took off his shoes inside the doorway, and made cat-like for the bedroom. Could have made all the noise he wanted. They wouldn't have heard him, all the noise they were making. Anyway, he stands just inside the bedroom door, the two of them—his wife and her boyfriend going at it to beat the band—and then he flips on the lights. His wife screams. The boyfriend, he jumps up buck naked and wide-eyed, staring down the twin barrels of the husband's shotgun. He looks at the gun, then at the husband. The husband smiles and fires off both barrels at the guy's crotch. The wife, she's screaming and going crazy. The husband reloads, shoots her too. Then he tosses the gun on the bed, switches off the light, and closes the door. Goes downstairs, pours himself a double whisky, calls the cops and sits down at his kitchen table, waits for the law to show up.

'When they got there he let them in, pointed to the bedroom. "You'll find them in there. What's left of them." He told them all about it, all the sad sorry details. The cops—they knew him, eh—they said "All right, Lenny, let's go" and Lenny says "Mind if I finish my drink. Last one I'll be having for quite some time." The one cop looks at the other, shrugs, says "Guess not." The other one picks up the bottle, tops off Lenny's glass. "Take your time. No hurry. They aren't going anywhere."

'But Lenny was.

'They sent him up for life.

'He was right, about that drink.'

'Did he ever get out?' Larry flicked his cigarette butt out the window.

'Let's say yes.'

'What do you mean "let's say"?'

'I'm not sure it's a true story,' I said. 'Some guy told me the story. Could be true. Could be one of those urban myths.'

'Beautiful,' said Larry.

There was a cool middle-of-the-night breeze coming in through the open windows. Didn't move a hair on Larry's head. Larry's head was slathered in Brylcreem. Gave him that nice Elvis-like sheen. We were looking at the skyline of Detroit—the part we could see between the corner of the Cleary Auditorium and the wall of the building which housed the Bandit's Café. Freighter throbbing past.

'Tough to imagine 'em sinkin', eh?' said Larry. 'But they do.'

'Yeah,' I said. 'The lakes can get pretty wild.'

'I'm not talkin' lakes,' said Larry. 'I'm talkin' the River.'

'Freighters?'

'Yeah. Freighters. Just like that one. Ever hear about the *Montrose*?'

'I shook my head.'

'Time to do a little homework, Hemingway. Head down to the morgue. Look it up. Pretty good story.'

Larry stubbed out his cigarette, grabbed his mop by the handle, and started pushing his wheeled bucket across the newsroom.

*   *   *

LARRY WAS RIGHT. THE SINKING OF *THE MONTROSE* FILLED UP A FILE FOLDER OF its own in a sliding drawer of one of the dozens of grey-metal filing cabinets in *The Star*'s morgue.

The gist of it was: Drivers should never pull out from a parking spot without checking the traffic. Captains shouldn't either. But the captain of the brand new Canadian-owned British freighter *Montrose* did just that late on the night of July 30th, 1962. Unluckily, he pulled directly into the path of a cement barge being pushed downriver by the tugboat *B.H. Becker*.

The barge tore a huge hole in the *Montrose*, the ship's bow began to sink, its propellor lifted out of the water, the currents carried it downstream and it went aground under the Ambassador Bridge. The crew of 38 was rescued.

It took a salvage firm two months to raise the Montrose and tow her away for repairs. So for two months, Windsor and Detroit had another tourist attraction: Thousands lined both shores to look at the wreck. Traffic slowed to a crawl on the Ambassador Bridge as motorists rubbernecked. The Boblo boats reported a 20-percent increase in business as passengers sought a closer view of the wreck. The cruise boat *Dee Cee*, moored at Detroit's Civic Center, made special trips around the *Montrose*. Bridge officials barred pedestrians from the Ambassador Bridge after 8 PM, fearing for their safety.

'The river's beautiful to look at. But dangerous at times.' Right again, Larry.

An abbreviated list:

October 9 1854: The steamer *E.K.Collins* left Detroit between 10 and 11 PM. An hour later she was in flames below Amherstburg.

Thirty-four were rescued, but twenty-three died, either in the flames or in the river.

July 22, 1880: The pleasure steamer *Garland* collided with the steam yacht *Mamie* just below Grassy Island (the island on the American side of Fighting Island, opposite LaSalle), killing seventeen of the twenty-four on board.

September 2, 1891: The steam barge *Jenks* turned into the path of the steam barge *George W. Morley* near Ballard's Reef. The wife of the *Jenks*' captain, the engineer and fireman, all below deck, were killed. Six were saved by the crew of the *Morley*.

July 31, 1894: The whaleback steamer *Pathfinder* struck and sunk the small schooner *Glad Tidings* a few miles below Detroit at 1:30 in the morning. All four aboard the schooner died.

August 15, 1916: The 445-foot steel-hulled freighter *Topeka* collided with the 228-foot wood-hulled coal steamer *Christopher* in dense fog just off the Mullen Coal docks in Sandwich. The *Topeka* sank in forty feet of water, but all 20 crew were saved.

June 18, 1936: The *Tashmoo*, an elegant old cruise ship, hit a rock near Grosse Isle while on a midnight cruise. The orchestra played on while the captain called for full speed ahead. He managed to dock at the coal wharf above Amherstburg. Passengers and crew watched from the wharf as the *Tashmoo* settled to the bottom in 18 feet of water.

SOME ENDINGS ARE LESS DRAMATIC.

The *Aquarama*—one of the ships Doug Todd remembered—was briefly one of the queens of the Great Lakes. She was 520 feet long, 71 feet wide, had nine decks and carried a crew of 189. She carried as many as 2500 passengers at 22 miles an hour and did so in style. There were gift shops and games arcades, two dance floors, a movie theatre, five bars, four restaurants and a 300-seat cafeteria.

When I first saw her, she was a rusting hulk moored for a year or so in a slip near the foot of Mill Street.

Still elegant, but pathetic.

The ship was built in 1945, made one trans-Atlantic run as a troop ship, then sat unused until 1952, when new owners spent $8 million over the next two years transforming her into a sort of ocean liner for the Great Lakes. Sounded like a great idea. The ship began touring the Great Lakes in 1956, making regular runs between Detroit and Cleveland, but never made a profit. She spent a quarter century tied up in Muskegon until new owners moved her briefly to Sarnia, and then to Windsor, where she was a gawker magnet.

She was towed to Buffalo in 1995 and finally scrapped in 2007.

*　　*　　*

THE ADVANTAGE OF LIVING IN AN ATTIC ON OUELLETTE AVENUE WAS THAT ... well, there were a couple of advantages.

One: Go across the road, down the ramp to the emergency department, go through the sliding doors and down the hall to the cafeteria. Open all night. Everything fairly tasty and very cheap. And all those young nurses to chat with.

Two: Go a few doors north, knock on a certain door, and say hi to One-Eyed Louie.

'Come on in.'

Louie was the now-and-again boyfriend and guard dog at Mary Mary's, one of those quiet little after-hours spots where you could find a drink, a card game, or a little companionship of the female variety. I limited myself to the drinks, though the card games looked interesting, and the females were always smiling.

One-Eyed Louie sat in a big arm chair just inside the door. Charming in a greased-down thuggish kind of way, although the big bulge his 'peace-keeper' made under his jacket was a little unnerving.

Louie and Mary were an item. Whenever he wasn't in jail—'Louie? He's away just now.'—he was at Mary's, keeping the peace.

The last time he was 'away' he'd robbed a bank.

Went in with a toque over his head, pointed the peace-keeper, demanded the cash, made the getaway. He was back in his little basement flat counting the take when there was a knock on his door.

'Hi Louie.'

'Well, hello officers.'

They looked at the pile of cash. They looked at Louie.

'How'd you know it was me?'

'You had a toque over your head?'

'Yeah.'

'Let's see the toque, Louie.'

Louie handed them the toque.

He'd cut an eyehole.

Just the one.

As they saw, not the sharpest knife in the drawer, but Mary loved him so there he sat, making sure things remained peaceful and profitable.

The first time I went to Mary Mary's, there was quite a good crowd: A couple of guys I'd never seen before whose suits were worth more than everything in my closet, three reporters, one movie-theatre manager, one PR guy, two lawyers, one judge.

I looked at the judge.

The judge looked at me.

'I take it this is off the record.'

'Yes, your honour.'

*   *   *

MRS. MAJOR WOULD HAVE LIKED THOMAS REAUME. WHEN IT CAME TO THE history of Brighton Beach, Tom Reaume was a walking, talking textbook. A textbook that looked like he might have been a boxer at one time. Big shoulders, big hands. A knock on the front door of 4786 Scotten, and a solitary question—'I heard you might be able to tell me about The Brighton Beach Hotel?'—and the textbook opened right up.

Tom showed me into his kitchen, poured me a cup of coffee. I complimented him on his house. Big smile. 'Melba and I raised 12 children in this house. It was built just a couple of years before we moved in. The house that used to be here was destroyed by the tornado of '46. That tornado followed a path right up from the river, through this lot, then off into the woods on the other side of Seven Mile Road. Have a seat.'

We sat down at the kitchen table and away he went.

Tom's grandfather Albert John Reaume built The Brighton Beach Hotel. Actually, he put it together. The front half of the hotel was originally a building for a fish hatchery which once operated on the banks of the Detroit River ('Down near where Bob Pike had his house'). The back half was an old house. Albert John had the two buildings hauled to the site and nailed together. Later, an addition was built. Later still, he built a verandah around the whole affair, and he had himself a roadhouse.

We're talking turn of the century: 1901, or thereabouts.

Rules of the time stipulated that in order for a hotel to be licenced for the sale of beer, it had to be a hotel. Rooms to rent. So, upstairs at The Brighton Beach there were a dozen rooms, complete with beds. Fairly regularly a room got rented out. Occasionally for even an entire night.

Albert John lived in a suite of rooms above the bar. His son and the subsequent owner, Ernest Earl, later occupied the same apartment. Ernest Earl's son and the subsequent owner, Thomas, later occupied the same apartment.

From the time Albert John or Ernest Earl or Tom opened the doors (noon), until the time the doors were locked (midnight), and the place eventually closed (dawn, perhaps), The Brighton Beach Hotel, later renamed The Westwood, was a happening place. A couple of hundred people, sometimes more, were jammed into the joint. This was before the days of seating limits. 'When no one could move, you opened the verandah doors and people could dance on the porch.'

Tom's dad hired most of the well-known bands in the area: 'Brad Moxley, Rickie Johnson, Hec Renaud, Joe somebody, or Andy Donaldson 'the singing motorman,' who spent his days running trolleys in Windsor. The music was so good, and the place so popular, that CKLW Radio once considered running a wire down to the hotel so it could broadcast the dances live. But nothing ever came of that.'

In those days, there were a lot of bootleggers, and they all used The Westwood as their meeting spot. The rest of the clientele included hookers and cops, lawyers and business people, and folks from the neighbourhood.

'The lawyers were the worst of the bunch. Run up a tab and you'd have to chase them all over hell's half acre to get them to pay.'

'Do you have any snapshots?'

'Snapshots? I knew you were going to ask.'

But no, he has no snapshots of The Brighton Beach Hotel; no snapshots of his grandfather or his father or his uncle—the legendary Arthur J. Reaume.

A word or two about Art Reaume, Boy Mayor of Sandwich. He was elected mayor of the town at 24. When Sandwich was amalgamated with Windsor, he became a city councillor. Later he was elected, and re-elected, and re-elected again as Mayor of Windsor; later still, he became a Member of the Legislative Assembly.

As city mayor, he was, ex-officio, a member of the board at the municipally-run Metropolitan Hospital. Got a call one night from one of his pals saying there was a big party at The Book Cadillac Hotel over in Detroit. 'How's it going?' said Art. 'Lovely,' said his pal. 'Except we could use some female companionship.' 'Right,' said the Mayor. Next thing, a bus pulls up to the nurses' residence at Met Hospital. The Mayor encourages the student nurses to hop aboard. Next thing you know, there's all kind of screaming and mayhem on one of the upper floors of the Book Cadillac. Cops arrive and find all these men chasing all these student nurses around. Among those doing the chasing were cops and lawyers and other solid citizens from both sides of the border.

Art was also, ex-officio, a member of the police commission. And the commission took it on the chin for failing to notice that the city was riddled with whorehouses, blind pigs, and bookie joints. Eventually the whistle got blown. A provincial commission was held in 1950, and the feathers were in the fan. 'Scathing' would be a good adjective to describe the report, which demanded that things change. Things did. The police chief and deputy chief were forced to retire, and the Crown attorney was removed from office. The Mayor took it on the chin, but managed to survive one more election before moving on to greener pastures at Queen's Park.

Controversial and colourful would be two fairly apt adjectives.

But back to his nephew, Tom Reaume.

Tom had lots of snapshots, of course. Boxes of them. But you know how it is with old photos, eh? They have a habit of disappearing.

'Who knows where they all went? Hard to imagine you'd just throw them out.'

Nonetheless, they're gone.

'I've just got snapshots up here.'

Tom taps his temple with an index finger.

'There's a whole snapshot album up there.'

'Tell me more about your grandfather.'

'My grandfather?'

Albert John Reaume was a great pal of Bill Yawkey, the American who inherited ten million dollars from his lumber-baron father in 1903, and spent part of that money acquiring an estate in what is now Brighton Beach.

'You know where the propane fields are? On the far side of Sandwich Street, behind the sewage-treatment plant? That's where his house was. He had a couple of houses. A summer place down by the river, and that one.' Bill's summer house would have been right about where, 50 years later, the coal piles at the J. Clark Keith plant were. And the J. Clark Keith plant was right next to The Brighton Beach Hotel, which Albert John owned.

Bill Yawkey and his friend Frank Navin owned, among other things, the Detroit Tigers. Bill Yawkey's nephew and stepson, Tom Austin Yawkey, would later own the Boston Red Sox.

Anyway, there was a rail spur leading into the Yawkey property. Convenient. They could unload crates of booze from the rail cars and put them right into the buildings on the Yawkey property, then transfer them to the docks on the river. From there they'd make their way to the very dry and very thirsty U.S. of A. And Albert John became wealthy, and his pal Bill Yawkey became even wealthier.

As a boy, Tom and his pals would sneak down to the docks at night, and watch the American boats glide in, tie up at one of his grandfather's liquor docks, load up and slide out again, disappearing into the darkness with a throaty, burbly sound.

'There were four docks down there at the time.' Two of them were his grandfather's. One for liquor. One for beer. The liquor was shipped from the Hiram Walker distillery in wooden crates. Tom's grandfather and his workers would transfer the bottles to burlap bags—easier to load into boats—'then they'd sell the boxes to people for firewood.'

Enterprising. And, eventually, rich.

Albert John ended up with a lot of property. 'I don't think he went to school a day in his life. But he was very smart.' When he died—'Prohibition ended in '34, he died the following year.'—he left behind The Brighton Beach Hotel and a lot of other land and buildings and business interests besides. And cash.

Two of his four sons outlived him: Tom's father Ernest Earl, and Tom's uncle, the flamboyant Arthur J.

Ernest Earl got The Brighton Beach Hotel.

He and Arthur J. divvied up the rest.

When Tom was five or six, his parents split up. His father stayed on in the hotel—now known as The Westwood—living in the suite of rooms his father had once occupied. Tom, his mom and the rest of the family moved to a house in Sandwich, a mile or so down the road. Tom and his pals walked over to visit his dad and hang around all the time.

Back then, the area between Seven Mile Road (now Highway 18) and Sandwich Street was all the Yawkey estate. Fields and bush and vineyards. Sandwich Street extended right through to LaSalle and was called Old Front Road. Just beyond where the Morton Terminal slip is now, there were some old blast furnaces and craneways which were all that ever materialized of plans to turn Brighton Beach and Yawkey and Ojibway into a Canadian carbon copy of Zug Island.

Apart from that, there wasn't much along Old Front Road except farmers' fields and outbuildings, and an old Post Office.

I asked him what he knew of the history of Brighton Beach.

'It wasn't until the 1930s that people started building shacks down by the river' and the community of Brighton Beach was born. By the time Tom moved in with his dad at the hotel, there were about a dozen cottages down here on the riverbank, a few others inland on dirt roads. The area across Sandwich Street was still field and bush, still owned by Bill Yawkey.

'The Yawkey land was eventually sold to a real estate development company called Chappus Page Realty.' Wright Street is named after a family which owned a large farm in the area. 'What Yawkey didn't own, the Wrights did.'

The pilings for the J. Clark Keith power plant were driven in 1949, which Tom remembers because it was the same year his dad sold The Westwood. The power plant went online in 1953. Two years later,

Tom went to work there. Twenty-seven years later he retired. '1982, that was.'

We'd long since finished our coffees. Tom apologized, but he had errands to run.

I asked him if I could come back. Maybe see some of those snapshots, if he could find them.

'Any time. Come back any time.'

*   *   *

I thought this book was about the river.
It is, more or less.
What do all these characters have to do with the river?
Not much, he said. And everything.

*   *   *

I SAW AL DELANEY A FEW TIMES AFTER OUR LITTLE *TÊTE-À-TÊTE* AT THE DRAKE. On the streets. Down by the river. Checking the gutters, the little change chutes in pay telephones, the bases of parking meters. A couple of times our eyes met. He made like he hadn't seen me. Once, he saw me coming and crossed the street to avoid me. I wasn't in any hurry. And it wasn't something you could press.

Then one afternoon I was walking along Riverside Drive, just east of Ouellette. I was walking east, Al was walking west. He saw me. Looked at me like I was a stranger, and then he ducked into Stanley's. I followed him inside.

Everybody liked Stanley's. But it was on the dark side. You had to stop inside the door and let your eyes adjust to the lack of light.

Al had his back to the corner. He already had two beers on the table. One was a quarter down already. I caught the waitress's eye. 'Two draft.' I pulled back a chair at Al's table and sat down. I didn't ask him if it was all right. The waitress brought my beer. I looked at Al, smiled and said hi. He didn't respond. He sipped on his beer, put his glass down, and just looked at me for a moment. 'Yer harder to lose than the clap.'

We went through our ritual with beer and cigarettes. I didn't bring out my notebook right away. I left my cigarettes on the table. He helped himself. He'd just lit one up and looked at me. 'You really got me thinkin' 'bout all this stuff. Years 'n years I never thought about it much at all. Last couple of weeks I been thinkin' 'bout nothin' else.'

He shook his head. Smiled. 'Fought Tommy Loughran once. You ever hear of him?' I nodded. 'One of the best, Tommy was. Light-weight champ of the world. This woulda been '32, '33. Somewheres in there. Then he wants to move up, see? Packs on a little beef. Wants to go after the heavyweight title.'

'When you want to do something like that, you've got to get your-self some victories. So your manager goes shopping for grinders. Guys who can fight pretty good, but not great. Guys you can count on to give the crowd a show, but not beat the star.'

Loughran's manager had heard about Al. Then he saw him at work. He was impressed. Al's cut was twenty-five hundred. Same for his manager. 'This is '34 we're talkin' about. Thirty-four, '35. Big mon-ey, is what I'm sayin'.' The waitress put two in front of Al, and two in front of me, and carted off the empties. I was writing all this while. I just motioned for her to take what she needed from my pile of change on the table. And some for herself.

'And?'

Al was lighting a smoke off the tip of the one he'd just finished. 'Went ten rounds with him.' He stubbed out the butt and drew on his new one. Leaned back in his chair, like he was savouring it all over again. 'Ten rounds. Quite a surprise for Mister Loughran.' He gave me one of those schoolboy grins.

'After the fight, I goes up to him and says "Lemme see that left hand," and he says "What for?" and I says "Because I never seen it all durin' the fight. Jus' wanted to know what it looks like." He laughed, and the laugh descended into a cough, and it was a minute before he was back to normal.

'Problem was, I broke my right hand in that fight. An' my manag-er, Harry Alexander was his name, he sends me down to Miami to recuperate.'

It was down in Miami in '34 or '35 that Al Delaney met a broad named Daisy. 'Honest to God. That was her real name.' And she introduced him to a friend of hers. 'Charley Barleycorn, or whatever they call him.' We talked for a while about Daisy and Charley and the parties they had. The parties had gone on for quite a while. 'Prosperity! Whoooeee. It was in England where the money went to my head. Somethin' went to my head. I know the booze did.'

In one year, '37 or '38, he was fighting for eight, ten, twelve thousand a bout. 'Never less than twenty-five hundred.' By year's end he'd earned forty or fifty grand.

'I decided to take a little holiday in Paris. The franc was real low. I dunno. Four cents, somethin' like that. I wasn't there more'n six weeks an' I figger I went through four thousand bucks, forty-five hundred, somethin' like that. I musta gone into every bar in the city.'

And then he spent six weeks in Germany. 'The brothels—that's what they called 'em—were they ever somethin'. They even had champagne for ya when ya walked in. So you just sips your champagne while the girl comes walkin' out so ya can look 'em over. Like that. Real nice. So we partied around Germany, and went back to Paris, and then back to the States.'

Al had one elbow on the table. He was staring at his beer. It was as though he'd remembered something he hadn't thought about in years. Then it seemed he shook it off. He drew on his smoke and exhaled. He looked down at my notebook and then up at me. 'Where was I?'

'You went back to the States.'

'Oh yeah. Now this is funny. When I got off the boat in New York, I went into this bar. And who should be there but Al Roth. Promoter from New York. Al Roth! Hell, he didn't even drink. An' he's sittin' there with a highball in his hand. Last time I saw Al Roth was in London, before I took off for Paris. Set up some of my fights for me in England. I says to him, "Hey, Al, come to Paris with me. We'll have a time." But he says he don't want to come. He shows me these five bank books and says "That's where my money's goin'." So I left him there and took off for Paris. Anyway, here he is in New York with this real long face and I says "What's the matter Al?" an' he says "Remember them bank books?" an' I says "Yeah," an' he says "Well, someone beat me for it. All of it." '

Al raised his glass and then he set it back on the table. 'That's the point, ain't it? If ya got it, ya might as well spend it before somebody beats ya for it. He ended up with nothin'. I ended up with nothin'. Least I had a good time.'

No smile this time. Just a quick little shake of his head.

I was still writing when he stood up. He finished the last of his beer and set the glass down, bummed another couple of smokes, and buttoned his coat.

'Things were just getting interesting.'

He laughed. 'You got enough interestin' stuff in there to fill up a book.' He brushed his lapels, left side, right side, then headed for the door. He was about halfway there when he stopped and turned. 'I forgot yer name.'

I told him what it was.

'Yeah.'

I caught up to him on the sidewalk. He was standing there looking at the river, and at the skyline of Detroit.

'That's where it all started, eh?'

'Yeah,' he says. 'Seems like a lifetime ago.'

'It was,' I said.

'Yeah.' He shook his head. Looked at me, then turned and started walking toward Ouellette. 'So long,' he said. 'See you around.'

'Most likely,' I said. 'Small world.'

He laughed.

*   *   *

IT WAS ONE OF THOSE BEAUTIFUL OCTOBER DAYS——HOW MANY MORE beautiful days can there be in October?——when sitting inside seemed like sitting in jail. I grabbed my windbreaker and headed for the door.

'Where you goin', Hemingway?'

This was the City Editor, pipe clenched between his teeth. The pipe was always clenched between his teeth, except when he was drinking coffee.

'Out.'

'Could we be a bit more specific?'

'When I've got the specifics, I'll let you know.'

'So I should put this down as a scouting mission.'

'Exactly.'

'Well. Good luck, then. Something for tomorrow's paper perhaps?'

'If we're lucky.'

'Well. Good luck then.'

'You already said that.'

'You'll need all the luck you can find.'

I smiled.

He smiled, pipe and all.

I nipped into Lee's to see who was there. Benny Lee was there, behind the bar. He obliged with a couple of glasses. When I'd finished those he said: 'Two more?'

'Love to keep you company, Ben, but work calls.'

'Good luck with that,' he said.

That was three in a row. How could I not be lucky?

I used to run into Yorky downtown. Sometimes, if he had a few nickels in his pocket, you could find him perched on one of the stools at the Kresge's counter. If his nickels had run out, you could sometimes find him in the bus depot. The bus depot was fine, except they wouldn't let the bums hang around all that long, and they definitely frowned if anyone pulled a bottle out of their trench-coat pocket. So, spring, summer, and fall Yorky preferred to be out of doors, an alley perhaps, or down along the river somewhere. On a rainy day, you could sometimes find him in the mouth of one of the railway tunnels, doing his best to keep dry on the outside and lubricated on the inside.

He was always friendly and, if he was relatively sober, he could be chatty and very funny. And sure enough, twenty minutes later, who do I run into down by the railway docks?

'Hi Yorky.'

'Hello,' he said. Big smile, but there was a question mark on his forehead. 'I'm not sure we've been introduced.'

I held out my hand. Told him my name. Where I worked.

'Ah,' he said. 'That *Star*. Well, my pleasure.'

He was wearing the same trench coat he was wearing the last time I'd seen him, which was about three weeks earlier in Judge Stewart's courtroom. Stewart had done him the favour of sending him away until the end of the month. His pension cheque had arrived this very morning.

Anthony Quiller had told me that on the day of his release, Yorky would make a beeline for his favourite liquor store, the one down on University Avenue, that he had an amicable arrangement with the staff there. 'You should ask him about it.'

Seemed like a pretty good time to do so.

'Oh yes,' he said. 'Very amicable.'

The arrangement: The day his cheque came in, and he got out of jail, Yorky would sign over the cheque to one of his 'friends' behind the counter of the liquor store. The friend would advance him a couple of dollars, put the remainder in the till and note the balance on a sheet of paper, which was kept under the counter. In this way, Yorky could come in at his leisure, order his favourite, and have the amount credited to his 'account'. His favourite was Catawba, the wino's wine— 'come alive for a dollar five'—which was kept in a handy spot, right under the counter.

So, thanks to his pal Judge Stewart, he'd had a warm place to stay the last couple of weeks, and here he was in fine form. Judging by the bulge in his trench-coat pocket, he had been putting his cheque to good use.

He noticed that I'd noticed. He smiled, pulled the bottle—still in its liquor-store paper bag—from his pocket. 'May I interest you in a drink?'

'Just had a couple. But thanks anyway.'

'Perhaps we should go over there,' said Yorky, indicating the mouth of the railway tunnel. 'It doesn't do to draw attention.'

'Of course.'

So we repaired to the mouth of the tunnel, stood there looking out at the river and the skyline of Detroit. Yorky helped himself to a little wine, screwed the cap on, and put the bottle back in his pocket. He was smiling. Then he started laughing. Giggling, actually.

'What's so funny?'

'One time I was down at the store (the liquor store over on University), standing outside with this fellow I didn't really know all that well. I said to him: "I'm going in to get a bottle." The fellow, he says: "You got any money?" I said to him: "No. I'll just charge it." "Charge it?" he says. "Are you kidding?" "Oh no," I said. "I do it all the time. I have an account here." "Bullshit," he said. "Well," I said, "what about a little wager?" "Sure," he said. "How much money have you got?" I asked. He checked his pockets and put all his change in the palm of his hand, counted it out. "Dollar twenty-seven," he said. "All right," I said. "I wouldn't want to take every last cent. How about a dollar?" "All right," he said. "All right," I said, "I'll bet you a dollar that I can walk in there, go up to the counter, order my usual and have them put it on my tab." "You're on," he said.'

Yorky has a devilish little smile about this deep into the story.

'So, I walk up to the counter and say "Hi" to Bruce, and he said "Hi Yorky" and I said "I'll have my usual" and Bruce pulled a bottle from beneath the counter and put it in a brown paper bag and handed it over. "Just put it on my tab," I said. "Certainly, Yorky." So we go outside and this fellow, he said: "Well, I'll be damned," and handed over a dollar. He looked at me, then down at my bottle in the bag, and then through the door. He said: "I'm going to give it a try."

'So in he went. "Hi Bruce," he said. "I'll have one of whatever Yorky just got. And you can put it on my tab as well."

' "Beat it," said Bruce.

Yorky can't help himself. He's giggling and snorting.

'What he didn't know, of course, is that I deposit my pension cheque at the liquor store every first of the month, and just keep charging the bottles until my account comes up empty.'

'And you'd forgotten to mention it to him?'

'Apparently,' he said.

We both laughed.

'Well,' he said. 'I must be off. Places to go, people to meet.'

'See you around.'

'Quite likely.'

*   *   *

SOMETIMES LATE AT NIGHT I'D FIND MYSELF STANDING BY THE RIVER railing just staring at Detroit. Thinking. Wondering. Puzzling. Another world over there. You have to admit, it's a little weird to look at Detroit from our side of the river. Back in the '60s, Detroit had a million-and-a-half residents. It was the fifth largest city in the U.S. And there I was, standing in a rinky-dink little border town, sidewalks all rolled up, staring at it. Right at that moment, a mile or less away, there were hundreds of thousands of people I'd never meet and never know, doing all kinds of things I'd never hear about: Out partying or playing poker in the middle of the night in some little downtown hideaway, or people being shot or mugged or—on a steamy Sunday night, July 23rd, 1967— going crazy. Looting, shooting, burning. The whole town gone nuts.

And there I was, standing at the river railing, watching the evil glow of fires here, there, and everywhere, just back of the riverfront wall of office buildings. I could smell the smoke and hear the sirens. What I wouldn't have given to be over there with my notebook and pen. Except I was trapped right where I was, on the Windsor side, the border sealed shut.

Wait a minute, she said.

What?

I thought you said you covered the riots.

I did?

Yeah. Someone asked if you were around at the time of the riots and you said, I'm quoting here, 'I covered the riots.'

I said that, eh?

You said you and this reporter friend of yours, Kevin someone, got through the tunnel just before they closed the border and you spent all night filing all these great stories.

I said that?

You did, she said.

AH, MEMORY. THERE'S A TRICKY OLD GAL.

I did say that. But the really eerie thing is I *thought* I covered the riots. I can remember the Detroit riots so clearly. I can actually see the street scenes: Shattered windows, looters running with their arms full, cops hollering warnings, shots fired from rooftops. A black-and-white film, complete with soundtrack. When it came around to writing this section of the book I thought it would be fun to go back through *The Star*'s files and see what kind of little gems I'd produced. So I went up to the second floor of the downtown public library, where they have all the old *Windsor Star* microfilms. I pulled out the reel for July 1967. Scrolled through. Couldn't believe it. Scrolled through again. Ken Campbell's byline was there. Kevin Doyle's. Cec Scaglione's. Walt McCall's.

Jeezus, how could I remember it all—*remember it all*—so clearly, and yet not have been there?

You want weird? That's weird.

What in hell was going on?

I sat there looking at those old stories, and then it came back to me, vaguely at first, then in more detail. What really happened: I'd gone up home to Southampton that weekend, and got a call Sunday morning from my pal Kevin Doyle:

'Vase, you gotta get back here. Right now.'

'What's happening?'

'What's happening? Haven't you been listening to the radio? Detroit is burning.'

'Detroit?'

'They're rioting. The whole fucking town has gone crazy. You gotta get back here. Right now.'

'It'll take me four hours to get there. Four or five.'

'Well, haul ass. I'll see you when you get here.'

But by the time I got there, they'd sealed the border. And Kevin was nowhere to be found.

But there I was, smelling smoke, listening to sirens. Trying to imagine what was going on right before my eyes. And for the next few days, like everyone else in town, I looked over at the plumes of smoke above Detroit. Read the news stories. Listened in Lee's and the Press Club as the reporters who'd actually been there told us, detail for detail, what it was like.

Somehow or other I just absorbed all those details and made them mine.

This does make you pause. And it does make you contemplate the nature of memory. And you have to finally conclude that memory, at the very least, is unreliable. We have an ability, like Toad of Toad Hall, to dress things up, just a teensy bit. We adjust a fact here, delete a fact there, until the story 'feels' right and 'sounds' right. And then it *is* right. And it really happened. We do this all the time.

I can't remember the number of times we've been at a party, or sitting with friends around the dining-room table, and I'll be telling a story, and the brown-eyed girl waits 'til I'm done (sometimes not) and mentions 'that's not the way it happened.'

It's not?

No.

She then fiddles with the details until they correspond more properly with her recollection. Which, of course, may or may not be accurate. But you don't get to be married to the same woman for 40-something years by pointing these things out.

It's my habit, in such circumstances, to refill my glass, retire to my corner, and think things through. Sift through the details as *I* remember them. Sort things out, make a few adjustments. Add something here. Delete something there. Tinker with the chronology.

There.

'Okay, so this is what really happened …'

Jeez, she said. Can we trust anything in here?

Of course, he said.

If you can't even remember whether you covered the Detroit Riots, how are we supposed to believe anything you put down?

Well, he said. You should never let a few facts get in the way of a good story.

I can't believe I'm hearing a newspaperman say that.

I'm not a newspaperman any more, I said.

So what are you?

A teller of tales.

Factual or not?

Some of each, he said.

But which ones are which?

Hard to tell, he said. Does it matter?

I SUSPECT WE NEVER REALLY GET ANYTHING STRAIGHT. WE JUST KEEP WRITING and rewriting our stories until they have a little music and they have a little magic. If they *feel* right and *sound* right, that's probably as close as you'll get.

A dash of fact, a splash of fiction. Presto: A story.

Remember what Norman Levine said back there at the beginning about life, once lived?

The key question: Is it a good story? Does it keep you turning the pages?

The other key question: Is it true?

Because, after all is said and done, that's the only thing that matters.

HOWEVER, IF YOU'RE A STICKLER FOR FACTS ABOUT THE DETROIT RIOT, here's what happened, according to *other people's* news stories.

The 12th Street neighbourhood, as they referred to it at the time, was a 'Negro neighbourhood,' which, reading between the lines, meant it was not an area you'd want to wander into even before July 23rd. It was noted for its crime rate. Just before four in the morning on Sunday the 23rd, cops from the 10th precinct raided a blind pig in a dingy building at 9215 12th Street. Within an hour, the cops had rounded up more than 70 people, cuffed them, and taken them down the stairs to the street, loading them in waiting paddy wagons for the trip downtown.

The word on the street was that the cops had shoved a handcuffed teenager down the stairs. Not true. But the story, and the outrage, spread. Crowds began to form.

Then, just before five in the morning, someone tossed a bottle.

Within moments, the crowd began to move down 12th. More bottles flew, windows were shattered, people began stealing whatever they could get their hands on through those broken windows.

Liquor stores were a popular target.

A little after five in the morning, the police switchboard lit up. Twenty past five, Police Commissioner Ray Girardin woke up to a ringing phone. A couple of minutes later, he was on the phone to Mayor Jerome Cavanagh. By six, the police chief was in his office trying to get a handle on things.

There were no handles.

By 6:30 the first fire—in a 12th Street shoe store—was reported.

As Gordon Lightfoot would famously put it: Black Day In July.

Monday morning, July 24th, at least four were confirmed dead and there were 800 injured, including at least 23 policemen and six firefighters.

Governor George Romney asked President Lyndon Johnson to send in 5,000 troops. There were 10,000 police officers and National Guardsmen on the streets, and they were unable to put the genie back in the bottle in the 'Negro neighbourhoods' of northwest Detroit. The riots had now spread from one neighbourhood to the next and, by Sunday night, it had spread right downtown.

There was looting, firebombing, and sporadic gunfire seemingly everywhere.

The thirteen blocks of 12th between Atkinson and Bethune were a nightmare of smouldering or flaming buildings. Rioters were making off with everything they could lay their hands on: Groceries, clothes, and liquor.

By Monday, more than a thousand people had been arrested. Whole blocks of homes and shops had been destroyed by fire. Snipers were trading shots with cops and national guardsmen.

The National Guard ordered five tanks and two armoured personnel carriers into the heart of the riot area on the near-west side, three miles from downtown. The guard said police sharpshooters were firing from helicopters on rooftop rioters.

The U.S. border was closed at 9 PM Sunday. Monday, Canadians attempting to cross the bridge or go through the tunnel to get to their jobs in Detroit were turned back. Truckers trying to bring parts to Windsor's auto plants were refused entry on the American side. Chrysler had to cancel its shifts.

And just as they did on Fireworks Night, Windsorites flocked to the river to watch the sky glowing red above Detroit's west side as more than 70 fires blazed in the riot-stricken area. Riverside Drive was a virtual parking lot as cars jammed the Drive between Ouellette and Huron Line.

It was a tale of two cities: As northwest Detroit was burning, a crowd gathered in Dieppe Gardens for an outdoor concert.

When it was over five days later, 43 were dead, nearly 1,200 injured, more than 7,200 arrested and more than 2,000 buildings had been destroyed.

*　　*　　*

ART DAVIDSON ONCE TOLD ME 'EVERYONE'S GOT A STORY. IT'S YOUR JOB TO get them to tell it.'

Sometimes it doesn't even take a question to get people talking.

'Ever hear of the Purple Gang?' Anthony Quiller and I were back at our usual meeting place: The counter at Kresge's. Burger for me. Grilled cheese for him. Milk for both. Total bill less than a buck.

'No,' I said. 'Never heard of them,' I said.

'Pretty notorious murder-and-mayhem Detroit mob back in Prohibition Days. Left a trail of bodies everywhere they went. You should check them out,' he said.

'I'll do that,' I said.

'And then you should go see this client of mine. He used to work for them.'

'He did? You can set things up?'

'Of course.'

About a week or so later—wrong turn, right turn—I'm heading down a little two-rut lane that led to a canal that led to the Detroit River. A black four-door '58 Pontiac parked beside a little white-and-rust house trailer, parked beside a weathered, unpainted boathouse that was listing a little to starboard and looked like one strong wind would bring it down.

And there was Dick Trout—late 60s, ball cap, beer gut, three days growth—sitting on a lawn chair with a cigar in one hand and a coffee mug in the other.

I introduced myself.

'I know who you are,' he said.

'I was wondering …'

'… about the Purple Gang.'

'Yes.'

'Well,' he said. 'I suppose we ought to get you a mug with a little something in it before we get down to all that.'

'Thanks,' I said. 'But I just finished a coffee.'

'Who's thinking coffee?' he said.

So there we were, on either side of the table in the kitchen of his trailer: Two coffee mugs, one bottle of Hiram's finest. No ice.

'You worked for the Purple Gang?'

'I did indeed. Drove boats for 'em. Fixed boats for 'em. Hid a couple of the gang members right here a couple times. That old boathouse right there.' He tapped the window beside him. 'You do any homework before you came here?'

'Some,' I said.

The homework: The Purple Gang controlled the illegal booze business in Detroit during Prohibition. Very lucrative. By one estimate there were more than twenty thousand blind pigs in Detroit alone.

'They were just a bunch of Jewish kids,' said Dick. 'The Bernstein brothers. Abe and Joe. Izzy and Ray. It was Ray I worked for, mainly. Crazy little sonofabitch. So it was the Bernsteins and some of their friends.' The boys had got their start like all good little gangsters: Beating up kids and taking their money, busting store windows and threatening worse unless the owners paid for protection.

'They were murderers and thugs,' said Dick. 'They were tough and they were vicious. And a little bit crazy. You wanna know how tough they were?'

'How tough?'

'Even Al Capone wouldn't mess with them. He was thinkin' of maybe movin' into the Detroit scene, and what he knew of the Bernsteins, he said to hell with that. Teamed up with them instead. They were kinda like his local agents. So that's how tough they were.

'Let's put it this way. It's kind of a surprise I'm still here talkin'.'

'Why'd you work for them?'

'Five hundred a job. This is the 1920s we're talkin' about, sonny. Who wouldn't work for them?'

'Tell me about the job.'

'Well,' said Dick. 'How's your drink?' He was topping his off. Then topped mine off before I could say 'fine'. 'This one time Ray, he says he'd like to see me. Come on over, he says.

'What these guys were doing, they were hijacking other people's booze. They never bothered with small-time smuggling. Wasn't enough in it. They'd just show up and take truckloads of booze belonging to the smugglers. And boatloads. And, of course, all the cash that could be found in the immediate neighbourhood of the trucks and the boats.

'Which is where I came in. How's your geography?'

'Failed it twice. Grade 9 and Grade 11.'

He laughed. 'Well, that there is Fighting Island.' He pointed at the island we could see at the end of the canal. 'Hang a right out the end of the canal, go around Fighting Island, cross the river and you're in Wyandotte, Michigan. Wyandotte, Michigan, there's all kinds of cuts and canals, and Ray said in one of them canals there was going to be a boat unloading some booze, and the job was, we zip in, grab the booze, grab the cash from the boys who were waiting for the booze, load the booze and the cash in the boat and hightail it up the river to another cut where he's got his own truck waiting.'

He smiled, had another sip from his mug. 'He said these guys, they might be a little reluctant to agree to the transaction. So Ray says "I'll come along. And I'll bring my friend Tommy to do the convincing." They were reluctant all right. This one guy, real tough guy, points his gun at Ray and tells him to bugger off. Fires a couple of warning shots at my boat. Ray wasn't a big believer in warning shots. He put a few holes in this clown. The rest of them either dove in the water or took off runnin'. We took the booze and the cash and hightailed it up the river. Ray gave me an extra hundred to fix the bullet holes in my boat. Which is right out there,' said Dick, pointing at the boathouse 'Wanna see it?'

He added a little whisky to his mug and a little to mine and we crossed the yard to the boathouse.

It was a beauty. Mahogany. Twenty feet long. Red leather seats. Chrome fittings. 'Don't make 'em like this no more.' We stepped down into the boat. He lifted the hood of the engine compartment. 'Nice little four-cylinder. Out of a Ford roadster. Still works like a charm.' He pointed to a couple of small patch-jobs on the deck in front of the windshield. 'There's those hundred-dollar bullet holes.'

'You ever get arrested?'

'Nope. Chased up and down the river. Shot at quite a few times. But never collared.'

'How long you work for them?'

'All through Prohibition. Well, almost. They didn't quite make it all the way through, as you know from your homework.'

Homework. Part Two.

The Bernstein Brothers were nasty and smart. They mostly targeted other gangs of thieves, and the cops didn't mind if one gang of thugs killed off a few rivals. Lightened their workload. And even if the cops rounded up a few gangsters who survived the shootings and beatings, those guys knew better than to say a word to the cops.

The Purple Gang arrived at the end of the road in the fall of 1931.

What happened was, three small-time thugs got themselves in trouble. They were running a bookie outfit in Detroit and couldn't pay when one of their customers won a big bet. So they bought some booze from The Purple Gang, watered it down and began selling it at bargain basement prices. The Bernsteins did not appreciate the competition. They invited the three small-timers to a meeting. Only the Bernsteins left the room.

The Wayne County Prosecutor said it was the last straw. He wanted the Bernsteins 'dead or alive.' By this time, The Purple Gang had so many enemies it didn't take the cops long to find someone willing to talk. And within two days of the slaughter, they had most of the members of The Purple Gang in jail. A month later, three of them— Ray Bernstein, Irving Milberg and Harry Keywell—were sentenced to life without parole and shipped off to prison in Northern Michigan.

The rest of the gang disappeared or wound up full of holes.

And that was it for The Purple Gang.

'Another drink?' said Dick.

Well, why not?

*   *   *

BRIGHTON BEACH. COULDN'T STAY AWAY. EVERY NOW AND THEN, NOTHING else to do, I'd swing past Bronson's Tavern (the old Brighton Beach

Hotel) for a little knock-knock and a chat. Well, didn't always swing right past.

One day, after having just the one, I drove around the neighbourhood, saw an old fellow walking from his house at Scotten and Broadway, heading for a little backyard shack.

Seemed like a driveway I should park in.

The fellow's name was Archie Jamieson. He and his wife Ivy had lived in that house since 1957. Neat little bungalow, clad in greenish vinyl. There was an Olds coupe in the drive and, alongside it, Archie's white-and-red Ford pickup with a tell-tale powerlift gate.

Archie's father never lived in Brighton Beach. But he did buy 17 lots (approximately 25 feet by 100) paying, Archie seems to recall, 'about three or four hundred for the whole bunch.' Archie's father was a plasterer and the land looked to him like it might turn a tidy profit years down the road. This was back in the War Years. Or maybe just before. Then Archie's father suffered a stroke and that was it for both plastering and speculating.

When Archie's dad died, he owed about six hundred dollars in back taxes on his holdings in Brighton Beach. Six hundred dollars was about five hundred and fifty more than Archie could lay his hands on at the time. So the land was divvied up: Some lots to one of his aunts, some to one of his uncles, and this corner lot to Archie. 'My uncle was no fool. He didn't want the corner lot. Taxes on both frontages.'

Archie and Ivy contracted a builder.

So there's the history.

Archie Jamieson's backyard was filled with retrievables. Like his neighbour Andy Todd, Archie went around in his pickup retrieving the good stuff before the city boys hauled the rest of the garbage out to the dump. Archie carted his stuff home, stacked it in his yard and waited for customers to show up.

Right behind the house, there was a little red-painted clapboard shack. Lock on the door. Inside, Archie had a homemade can crusher (an inverted car jack: Three or four cans crushed in one squeeze) and an oil barrel full of squished pop cans, which kept Archie busy and in spending money.

'You know where this shack comes from? This shack came from Ojibway.'

Ojibway?

'You know. Over there. On the far side of the bush.' He pointed across the road. 'Used to be a town all its own. This is an old police shack. The shack where the cops stood by the side of the road looking for speeders or whatever. This shack must be a hundred years old.'

When the cops no longer wanted it, Archie and a friend struggled the shack up onto the back of his pickup, and transplanted it here in his back yard.

I asked Archie if he'd always been in the recycling business.

No. Not always. Not exactly. But he had always been of an entre-preneurial spirit.

Back during the Second World War, booze and cigarettes and all kinds of other essentials were rationed. Everyone wanted sugar. Not everyone wanted the weekly allotment of beer and liquor.

Archie Jamieson was—how shall we say?—well-connected. He would make the rounds, picking up those of little thirst and taking them in his own car down to the local outlet. He'd wait in the idling car, while his passenger went in and bought the permitted bottle of whisky or case of beer. Archie would drive the buyer home, give him what he'd paid for the booze, plus a tip of a dollar. Then on to the next buyer. When he'd made eight or ten trips to the outlet, he'd head for the Westwood (formerly The Brighton Beach Hotel), where Ernest Earl Reaume would gladly take the booze off his hands for a buck or two above what Archie had paid.

Would Archie qualify as a bootlegger?

Archie struck a thoughtful pose. 'No,' he said. 'I'd say I was more of, like, a delivery man.'

Ivy: 'His problem was he never made more than a dollar over what he paid.' Which is why Ivy and Archie are not millionaires living in one of those big bootleggers' mansions in Olde Walkerville.

Anyway.

One day there'd been a spot of trouble at the Westwood. Nothing serious. No one killed or anything like that. But the cops had been called.

Just as Archie pulled in to the parking lot and opened the trunk, a cop he knew came out the front door of the Westwood. 'I thought, oh oh, here we go'. But the cop came over to Archie's car, glanced in the loaded trunk, glanced at Archie and smiled. 'It's all right, Arch. We're all done. You can take the booze in.'

As soon as Archie stepped inside the front door of the Westwood, shouldering a gunny sack filled with whisky bottles, he spotted Art Reaume sitting at a table with just about the meanest cop in all of Windsor. 'And I figured oh, oh, here we go for sure.'

But no.

Art was, after all, the Mayor of Windsor. He was also, ex officio, a member of the Police Board. Art's brother Ernest Earl was standing behind the bar. He hollered: 'Bring that whisky over here, Archie. We've been waiting for it.'

Ivy and Archie, like most of their neighbours, spent a fair amount of time at The Westwood and never had any trouble getting in on a Saturday night. They'd walk right past all those people lined up to get in, and as soon as one the Reaume boys spotted them it was 'come on right in.' This had a good deal to do with Archie's status as a supplier of refreshments during the ration years of the Second World War.

Line-ups? At the Westwood?

Ivy: 'Oh yes. Every Friday and Saturday night. And the same up at The Lido (once upon a time The Chappel House, whose owner, Babe Trumble, was shot and killed by the pistol-packing, Bible-thumping liquor inspector J.O.L. Spacklin, self-appointed keeper of the public morals during those Prohibition years. Yet another story.)

'Anyway, The Westwood was the place to be in the early '50s. They had orchestras too.'

Archie: 'And good ones. Not all this country crap. Good music and a good hardwood floor to dance on. There wasn't an empty spot on the floor. No empty tables either.'

Ivy: 'And everyone was properly dressed. The women in dresses and the men in jackets and ties.'

Archie: 'Clean and decent. No holes in your clothes. No dresses up to your butt.'

And no trouble. Well, not a lot of trouble.

'Oh, they'd have the occasional fight.' But they also had Tommy Reaume working the door, and Tommy was built like a prize fighter.

I asked Ivy what she liked about the neighbourhood. 'When we first moved here, it was very, very nice. Very woodsy. There was a lot of bush and birds galore. Pheasants. We had pheasants right in the yard. Except when hunting season started. Then you wouldn't see one. They were smart.

'It was very nice.

'Crickets and frogs.'

I had a kind of weird feeling, leaving Ivy and Archie's place. It was like I'd just spent an hour with some relatives. You know, dropped in on a favourite aunt and uncle, sat with them at the kitchen table, got them talking all about family history. The way kids will, trying to figure out who did what and when, so that gradually, after visiting enough kitchens and drinking enough cups of coffee, you start to get a sense of who you are and where, in the grand scheme of things, you fit. Figure out your place in the world.

And I also got a sense that, if I was ever going to understand what the river *meant,* I would gain that understanding right here, in this forgotten corner of town.

When I first started nosing around, asking questions, I assumed I'd come across someone who'd open the door, tell me to scram, slam the door. But I hadn't been turned away from a single door. The people welcomed me and talked to me and they weren't anxious for me to leave. So far, not one Q&A session had gone less than half-an-hour. Most went an hour. A couple longer than that. It was like they'd all been waiting for me.

On my tours through the neighbourhood, I started waving at the people I'd already spoken with. They waved back and smiled.

Here's the strangest thing: I started to feel like I belonged.

And it did occur to me that I may have been sort of preordained to do this: To jot down these snippets of history and stitch them together eventually into some kind of fabric. Like a quilt. A word quilt.

It was fate I felt nudging me.

But the more times I drove through the neighbourhood, parked and walked across the body-dumping, trash-dumping field to sit for a while by the river, the more keenly I became convinced of it.

And, of course, I said nothing of this to anyone in the newsroom.

Not even Larry the janitor. Though Larry probably would have understood. He'd have fit right in down in Brighton Beach.

*   *   *

IT WAS MORE THAN A MONTH BEFORE I RAN INTO AL AGAIN. THE LAST OF THE snow had melted. Trees were budding. Noon hours you just wanted to be out in the sunshine. I made a habit on those bright spring days to go down by the river. I was down at the foot of Ouellette with my forearms on the railing. Then there were a couple of big hands out there next to mine, clasped like a preacher's. He said hello. He remembered my name.

'Haven't seen you around, Al.'

'Haven't been around.'

I offered him a smoke. He took two. He'd acquired a lighter. He cupped it in his palms and lit my smoke, then his own.

'Nice looking lighter.'

'Guy shouldn't leave a nice lookin' lighter on the edge of a craps table, should he?' Big laugh. 'Nice things, a guy oughta take a little more care of.' He flipped it up in the air. It would have been a straight drop right into the river. But he caught it and pocketed it. He was wearing one of those smiles.

'Got time for a beer?'

The question took me a little off guard. I hesitated for a few seconds. 'Sure.'

He turned and headed toward Riverside Drive.

'Lee's?' I said.

'Think I'm in the mood for somethin' a bit fancier.' He crossed Riverside and headed south. Next thing you know we're crossing the lobby of the Viscount Hotel, up past Hôtel Dieu, heading for the elevator. A guy came scurrying out from behind the counter. 'Excuse me, sir.' He stood between Al and the elevators. He was giving Al the once-over. Al was wearing a trench coat. An old one, shiny at the elbows, tattered at the hem. His trousers were rolled up. He was wearing sneakers. No socks. The manager was about to say something, but he missed his chance. Al slid around him and pressed the up button.

'Excuse me, sir.' The guy made the mistake of grabbing Al's elbow. Al turned so fast, he spun him right off. The manager maintained his balance, but barely. 'Touch me again, kid, I'll put your face right through the plate glass.'

The elevator doors opened on the 17th floor. Fancy little dining room they called Top Of The Town. Al walked right in. There was a guy standing beside a little podium where they checked your reservations. The guy looked at Al, then looked down at his bare feet in his sneakers. 'Excuse me, sir, but we have a dress code ...'

'Somethin' nice,' said Al. 'By the window. Lookin' over the river.'

The guy was about to say something, but by then Al was past him, heading across the dining room. He looked at a couple of tables, then decided on a table for four, right by the window. 'This'll do,' he said.

Now there were two manager types. Neither seemed especially pleased to see us. 'Excuse me, sir,' said the new guy. 'We have a dress code.'

Al gave him the once-over. 'You better spruce yourself up then.' Al pulled a chair back and sat down.

'I'm afraid you can't ...'

Al pulled a roll of bills from his pocket. Peeled off a five and clapped it in the manager's palm. 'Be a good boy. Fuck off and find us a waiter.' The manager looked at Al, then at the five-dollar bill, put the bill in his pocket and two minutes later a waitress showed up. All smiles and earnestness. 'May I help you?'

'You got draft?'

The waitress smiled. 'Yes. We do. Glasses or mugs?'

'Four glasses,' said Al. 'An' you can run us a tab.'

You could tell the waitress wasn't too sure about that. So Al pulled out his roll, opened it up and pulled out a fifty-dollar bill. He put it on the table and told the waitress to keep the beer coming. 'An' we'll have some lunch eventually. An' whatever we don't spend, you can keep.' He smoothed the bill out and folded it lengthways and put it the pocket of her apron. The waitress thanked him. Twice. The second time, she added a 'sir'.

'Rich aunt drop dead?'

Al grinned. He pulled a pack of cigarettes from the pocket of his trench coat. He opened the pack and offered me one.

'I've got some,' I said and reached for my own.

'Ain't every day I can offer.' He lit his own, then mine.

The waitress brought the drafts. Al ordered some pretzels. And some peanuts. 'An' a couple bags of chips while yer at it.' It wasn't until she'd come back with the goods and then left again that Al started talking. It was a long story. He'd got himself involved in a poker game. Win one. Lose a couple. Win a couple. Lose one. That kind of game. He was up fifty or sixty bucks, got a good hand and bet it all. One of the guys was out of money. All he had was a plane ticket. He was supposed to head to Vegas the following day. It was a round-trip ticket. 'So I tole him, toss it in, we'll play for that.' The guy thought about it for a minute or two. 'He looked at his cards and then he looked at me and finally he musta thought "what the hell." ' Al laughed. 'So three tens got me all the way to Vegas.' And a little luck brought him home with a couple of grand. I said that ought to keep him for a while. 'Day or two. Me'n money don't hang around together too much.' He set the lighter down and spun it around. 'Thing is, though, a roll in your pocket, there ain't no feelin' like it.' He looked up at me and grinned. 'Almost.'

We ate and had another smoke each. That was it for the first four beers. Al caught the waitress's eye. He made a circling motion with his finger. 'Them good times, they made me a sucker for every quick-buck proposition that come along.' The waitress put the fresh ones down at the edge of the table. She took away the wreckage of bags. 'But you know what they say, eh? Sounds too good to be true, usually is.' He raised his glass in my direction. 'Thing was, I never really believed that.'

I asked him what he meant. He said he was thinking about this time some years before, when he was staying in a little hotel in a country town. By the end of the evening he was pretty certain there'd be quite a stash of cash in the hotel safe. 'I had a gun. Only a toy gun, but it looked real enough.' Persuasion didn't work. The clerk kept saying there wasn't much money in the safe and, besides, the only one with the combination was the manager and he wasn't there. It was three in the morning. The manager was home in bed. 'So I says, "Let's go get him up." ' But just then a man appeared in the lobby. 'I'm wearin' a mask, see, an' this guy looks at me and says "What's this? Hallowe'en?" an' I says "Yeah," an' I slug him and down he goes.' The night clerk made for the door. 'My partner, he's in a pickup out front. He sees the guy runnin' out. That's enough for him. He took off. Left me standin' there. So I says, Al, I says, time to take a walk.'

Problem was, there weren't all that many six-foot-three men wandering around town wearing a genuine camel-hair topcoat, balaclava in one pocket, toy gun in the other. 'I got two years for that.'

The waitress had arrived in the middle of Al's story. She hung around to hear how things were going to turn out. When he was finished he looked up at her. Grinned. Sheepish grin. She just shook her head and smiled and away she went. 'Next time I was bouncin' cheques. Got three years for that.' His story took the usual turns. Break and enters. Crooked card games. Home repair operations. Blind pigs. All in all, he'd spent seventeen years in one jail or another. But all that was behind him now.

He looked out the window. Best view of Detroit you could imagine. Al was just staring at the skyline. 'That town,' he said. 'Love that town. Wasn't for that town, I wouldn't have amounted to nothin'. That one fight. Four rounds with Joe Louis. That was the ticket.' He shook his head. Smiled. 'Didn't do too bad for a small-town boy.'

'Not bad at all, Al.'

He spent the next few minutes staring out the window.

'Gonna haveta bring my lady friend up here sometimes. She'll love it.'

'Lady friend?'

'What time is it?'

I told him.

He finished his beer in one go. 'Gotta run.' He was on his feet now. The waitress arrived with four more beers. 'Be seein' ya, sweetheart. My friend here'll take care of them beers.' He patted her on the backside. 'You enjoy that tip.' She flashed him a big smile. Put the four beers down in front of me.

'Take yer time,' said Al.

Off he went.

* * *

I'M NOT MUCH OF A FISHERMAN.

When I think of fishing, I think of a story my pal Tom Latouf told me one time. He was fishing with two of his brothers. I should say that Tom is a big guy. And his two brothers might be bigger. So picture three big boys in a fourteen-foot boat as Tom tells the story.

'We were down by Sand Point Beach. There's a buoy about halfway between the beach and Peche Island and my brother threw out the anchor. Then we wanted to move and my brother he tried to bring the anchor in, but it was stuck. So he was pulling on the line and the harder he pulled the more the nose of the boat went down and—the current's really strong there, eh—the water started coming in. I looked around and, holy shit, the gas tank's floating and the boat's filling up. So my brother, he cut the anchor line and we started drifting. Next thing you know, we're down by the yacht club and we managed to grab onto the dock. We tied up there, tied the lines really tight so the boat wouldn't sink, and we bailed it out. Scary. We were that close to sinking. If we'd gone down in that current, who knows where we'd have ended up? No life jackets, of course.'

That's the kind of scenario that plays out in my mind when I think about going out on the river. Plus there's the question of sitting in a boat for four or five hours, tossing in a lure, reeling it back. Eventually, all that early-morning coffee would work its way through. And you know what they say happened to Tom Thomson when he stood up in his canoe and unzipped.

These thoughts apparently do not go through the minds of the thousands of people who head out in pursuit of walleye or perch or whatever else is lurking in the swift-running waters of the Detroit River.

If you're out early in the morning– spring, summer, fall—going to Tim's for your first coffee of the day, say, you'll see them on the road or in the parking lot: Pickups with a boat on the trailer. Sixteen, eighteen, twenty-footers, aluminum or fibreglass. Fishing nets

137

sticking straight up. Very cool. And some of them are pretty sophisticated: Swivel seat upfront, rod holders, fish finders, the works. (No bathrooms, however.) Some of them worth as much or more than the truck doing the hauling.

Beginning around dawn, sometimes earlier, you'll also see the fishermen zipping up and down the river, looking for the next best spot, or, if they've already found it, sitting with pole in hand while the boat drifts downriver. Now and then, they'll fire up the engine and head back up the river a little ways, then cut the engine and begin another slow drift.

They'll do this for hours.

And any time of day, any day of the week, you will find people standing by the river-railing, fishing pole in hand, big white water-filled plastic bucket by their foot, sometimes chock full of still-flipping fish, sometimes not.

My neighbour and buddy Tim Lefaive told me about his grandpa, who worked at Ford's. 'He told me guys used to go down to the river on their lunch breaks—this would have been back in the '30s—and throw a line in the river. Then they'd go back at the end of their shift and see if there was anything on the line. That's what you did back then—anything to put food on the table.'

People have been doing this since before there was a Windsor in the first place.

MOST ANGLERS ARE AFTER WALLEYE AND WHITE BASS, THE TWO MOST prevalent species in the river. The best guess—who knows how they count them—is that 10 to 12 million walleye reside in or move through the Detroit River each year. Yellow perch is a close third. Also small-mouth bass. And populations and catches of all those species, remarkably, have been on the upswing.

Other species: Crappies and bluegills, northern pike and largemouth bass. Now and then you'll hear of someone catching a muskellunge. And it's possible, though not likely, that you can hook a sturgeon. If you do, you'll get your picture in the paper. Lots of food for all those, apparently: Spot-tail shiner and other little nibblies in the water and lots of mayflies up above. The mayflies—or fish flies—

come in droves. Sometimes the droves have been so thick on River-side Drive that cars skid out of control and crash.

So despite the horror stories about the toxins and poisons that have been dumped—accidentally or otherwise—in the river, the abundance of fish seem to indicate that, somehow, Mother Nature has survived the assault.

Walleye can be caught from one end of the river to the other, but early in the season anglers say the best fishing is in the lower river, which warms faster than the upper and middle areas of the river. Lots of people like fishing up near where Tom and his brothers were that day, just off Sand Point Beach and the marina by Lilly Kazilli's.

A friend of mine and I were having a beer there one day when we saw two kids cruise into the marina in an 18-footer, tossing their lures into the corners, under the docks. Pinpoint. It was pretty cool to see. And when the boat got a little closer, I saw it was my pal Kyle Moxon who was up in the bow. Couldn't believe how expertly he could place a lure in the corner, under a dock. It was like he was throwing a dart at a target. But then he'd had a lot of practice. I think Kyle has been fishing the river since he was about five.

Some areas of the riverbank have been reinforced with riprap—big chunks of rock—and apparently the fish just love it. You can tell by all the boats parked right there. Fish also apparently love hanging around docks and seawalls, which accounts for all those kids standing along the park railings with a fishing rod, and people like my pal Kyle nosing their boats in around the docks in marinas.

There are fishing tournaments pretty well every weekend of the year (my buddy Kyle actually runs one). Want to see a sight? Head down to the river early on a Saturday morning (any time after five should do it) and just drink your coffee and wait. Suddenly boats will start racing up the river, dozens of them. All those guys (and women, too) have been waiting downriver for the starter's pistol. And when the tournament officially gets underway, it's a race to see who can get to the best spot.

Big business these days.

And lots of fun.

So they say.

PAUL VASEY

*   *   *

I ran into someone the other day who used to know you, she said.

Oh?

Didn't like you, she said.

Oh?

Said you used to be pretty full of yourself.

Me?

You, she said. 'Swaggering' was one adjective he used.

Me?

'Loud' and 'obnoxious' were a couple of others.

He may have mistaken me for someone else, he said.

Unlikely, she said.

As my ancient granny was fond of saying: If the suit fits, wear it.

So, yes, there were nights.

Press Club nights.

Add a little alcohol, light a flame.

This one night, the place was packed. People at the shuffleboard table, guys playing poker at the tables, guys lined up all along the bar. I'd wedged myself in between a couple of guys sitting on stools, put my foot up on the rail, ordered a whisky—'double, lots of ice'— and made myself comfortable. You know how things go: Next thing I know Val is giving me the eye as I'm ordering another double—not the 'I'm-about-to-cut-you-off' eye, but close—and I notice the crowd has thinned out. And somehow I'd found myself standing more or less nose-to-nose with an Ad Dink down the bar. Why did they let advertising salesmen in the *Press* Club, anyway? Ad guys liked to think of themselves as a part of the newspaper, but who could really believe that? As far as we were concerned, they shouldn't have been allowed in the Press Club in the first place. And if they were they should, like good little children, be seen and not heard.

You couldn't help but hear this guy. He was almost as loud as me. He was going on about this new 'product'. Something called adver-torial. Do you need to know anything more? Okay. Advertorial 101: Basically, an advertiser bought a whole page or a whole section and the Ad Dorks placed ads on the pages and then wrote all this treacly crap about the company. The crap was designed to look like news stories, headlines, photos, the works. Which made it seem as though *The Windsor Star* had completely lost not only its mind, but its moral compass as well.

I forget the exact words I used to tell him what I thought of his new 'product,' and precisely where he could shove it, but they weren't polite.

'What's the difference?' said the Ad Dork.

'What's the difference?' I may have been shouting by this point. Okay, I *was* shouting.

'There *is* no difference between advertising and news,' he said. 'It's all information for the reader.'

You may be wondering, in this age when there appears to be no line at all between advertising and the news, why I got so excited. But back then, there was a line. A huge black line. And nobody crossed it.

Mark Farrell, one of my all-time favourite *Windsor Star* publishers, had a little sign tacked to the wall of his office: *Comfort The Afflicted. Afflict The Comfortable*. Beside it, another one: *Lo, though I walk through the Valley of the Shadow of Death, I shall fear no evil because I am the Biggest Meanest Sonofabitch in the Valley.*

This would never have happened if Mark Farrell had still been with us. But Mark was gone, and the new publisher, hardly surprising, was an advertising guy who had floated to the top of the pond. And he thought it would be a great little money-maker if the ad department targeted little towns out in the county, went into Wheatley, say, and got every merchant to buy an ad on the premise that *The Star* would produce a whole section singing the praises of the town. He then told editorial to write the stories about the towns to *support* the ads. All positive, of course. We gagged. We cursed. As we saw it, the integrity of the newsroom was being attacked. And we, the reporters, had to make a last stand before we all ended up working for an ad agency.

You get the drift.

If memory serves, the Ad Dork said something like 'If it weren't for us, there wouldn't be any newspapers.'

'You are such an asshole,' I said. 'I can't believe I'm standing here talking to you.'

'Who's the asshole?' he said.

I can't believe I actually took a swing at him. The decibels were definitely rising.

It was at about this point in the proceedings that I felt a tap on my shoulder. There was a suit at the bar right behind me. Shirt, tie, slicked-back reddish-blond hair. I'd seen him at the bar before. We may have been introduced at some point. But the name escaped me. 'What do *you* want?'

He looked right at me. Tossed his business card on the bar. 'If you ever want to stop being a total asshole, give me a call.' He drained his whisky, got off his stool and headed down the stairs and out the door.

Guys were roaring.

'Who the hell was that?'

'You've got his card. That should tell you.'

I did have his card. Right there on the bar in front of me. 'Rod Scott' it said. 'Alumni Affairs Director. University of Windsor.'

Where the hell did he get off?

I went back to my argument with the Ad Moron. But after taking a shot like that, it wasn't easy to get back up on the high horse. I ordered another whisky. Uncle Val shook his head. 'You've had enough.'

'Screw you, I've had enough.'

'Go home.'

You didn't get told twice by Uncle Val to go home.

Next morning I was going through my pockets and there was Rod's card. I tossed it in the trash. Then I took it out of the trash and put it in my wallet.

Mister Scott and I would have to have a word one day.

*　　*　　*

IT WAS LATE JUNE NEXT TIME I SAW AL DELANEY. I'D BEEN LOOKING, BUT NO luck. The bartender at the British American heard he'd headed back to Vegas. Someone else heard he'd gone out to the coast. 'He's got a brother out there.'

It was nearly midnight. I was with a bunch of guys. We'd just come out of The St. Clair and wondered where to go next. I spotted Al across the street. He had an elbow up on a parking meter. It was like he was waiting for someone.

Then he headed down Wyandotte toward Ouellette. He was wearing a golf jacket, pale yellow. He had his hands in his pockets. He spread out his arms and it looked from a distance as though he'd grown wings. He was singing something. We couldn't quite hear the words. The guys I was with were heading over to The Tunnel Barbecue to get some ribs. 'I'll meet you down there.'

I crossed the street and followed Al. He was just strolling and singing. Not a care in the world. I was about half-a-block behind him. I figured, this time of night, he might be heading home. That was an address I wouldn't mind having. Al made a left on Ouellette. By the time I got to the corner, he was crossing the street. I picked up the pace, jogged across the street, got honked at, and made it to the far sidewalk just as Al was taking a right turn past the Vanity Theatre.

The building next to the Vanity used to be an apartment hotel. It was run by a vet from the First World War. He called it The Vimy. The name was in metal letters above the front door. Then the 'I' dropped off. The old vet never got around to putting it back up. Then he died. Someone else bought the place. They had the front painted. The painter didn't know any better. He removed the metal letters and then painted the name right on the wall. The VMY.

Al was standing in the doorway. He was kind of spreadeagled, feet wide apart, a hand on either doorframe. Then he pulled himself together and yanked the door open and went in.

'Sweet dreams, Al.'

I turned and headed for The Tunnel. I was starving.

Early next morning I was camped out on the sidewalk in front of The VMY.

The place had a reputation. Shootings. Knifings. But the most famous story was this time a guy was threatening to toss his girlfriend off the roof. The cops called the fire department. Told them to bring one of those big circular safety nets. Fire fighters arrived about two minutes late.

That's at night. In the morning, the place is like a tomb. Not a sound. No radios. No TVs. No hollering. Just the sound of your own footsteps. It's not the kind of place with a manager. You're on your own. And the mailboxes don't help. Most of them don't have doors and none of them has a name. Just the apartment numbers.

I figured I'd just wait him out. He'd have to come out sooner or later. And it was a nice sunny day. So I sat on the edge of the flower box out front and had a smoke and waited. An elderly woman was the first to come out of the building.

'Excuse me, ma'am. Do you know which apartment Al Delaney lives in?'

She might've been hard of hearing.

Three more people came out over the next half hour, but I was invisible.

Then the postman arrived. He wasn't too sure he should tell me information like that.

A dollar bill changed his mind.

Top floor. Apartment 3A.

'And you don't know how you found out.'

'Never seen you in my life.'

Three minutes later, I put an ear to Al's door. Not a sound. The night he had, I figured I was safe for half-an-hour, maybe more. There was a little diner just up Ouellette. I nipped in there for breakfast. Read the paper.

Forty five minutes later I knocked on his door.

Knocked again.

Took him a few minutes of fumbling around—'Who the fuck is it?—to get to the door. He opened it. Held onto it. Focused on me. Told me right away what he thought of me. He never had liked me, right from the start. And that was just the start. When he was done he turned and made his way back to his bed. But he just sat on the edge of it. And he hadn't slammed the door in my face.

I walked in. Closed the door. I pulled out my smokes.

'You got a search warrant?' He grabbed three cigarettes. Then he took another for good measure. He put three on the night table, the other between his lips. I lit it for him.

I cleared some of his clothes off the only chair in the room. Sat down.

'Make yourself at home.'

I sat and had a smoke. He didn't say anything until he'd finished his second cigarette. 'I thought I was all done with you.'

'I just had one more question.'

He looked at me and shook his head. Reached for another smoke. He was back to matches. It took him a couple of tries to get fired up. 'I ain't answerin' nothin' 'less you get me a coffee. Big and black.'

I was just pulling the door open.

'Maybe won't answer even then.'

When I got back he had his pants on. But he was still on the edge of the bed. He'd found his own smokes. He was almost finished another one. He ran a hand through his hair and took the coffee. He set the cup on the table and worked the lid off. He had to use both hands to bring it to his lips. I was in the chair again. He didn't acknowledge my presence until he was almost finished the coffee.

'What question?'

I told him.

He looked at me and shook his head. 'No.'

He finished his coffee, crumpled the cup and tossed it on the floor. Another drag and his cigarette was finished. He took a final look at it, as though to check, then stubbed it out in the ashtray. 'Any time I feel bad I just think of Al Roth. Al Roth and his bank books.'

He looked at me. I didn't say anything. I wasn't writing. I just sat there with my legs crossed and took another draw on my cigarette. He shrugged. Made a grimacing motion with his lips. 'I'm not pleased with my career. Hell.' He laughed. 'It wasn't a career. It was an escapade. But mostly I'm not pleased with bein' broke.' He was down to his last cigarette. He tossed the pack across the room. Lit up. He waved out the match, but held onto it between thumb and forefinger. 'Hell. I coulda been heavyweight champ of the world. I had the ability. I just wasn't serious. Only things I was ever serious about was women'n booze.' I still wasn't saying anything. When he was done his smoke he just dropped it in the ashtray. 'Only way to make it in this business is to live like a priest.' He smiled. 'I sure's hell wasn't no priest.'

We sat there for another couple of minutes. He was thinking about something. He almost started to speak and then he changed his mind.

He reached toward the night table where the cigarettes had been. I tossed him my pack. It fell between his hands. He leaned down and picked it up off the linoleum floor. He scratched the back of his neck. He was leaning right over, looking down at the floor.

'There's only one thing.' He was talking softly now. 'I had a girlfriend once. A real girlfriend. Me'n her went out a long time. Years 'n years. It was kinda off an' on with her. I dropped in when times weren't so good. Name was Dolly.' He flicked his ash onto the floor, then brushed it away with his foot. 'This one time I pulls in in the middle of the night. I was down to my last five bucks. I remember thinkin', I can't lose this fin. Anyways, Dolly lets me in an' gets me into the tub an' takes all my stuff and next thing you know I'm all cleaned up and there I am in bed in clean pajamas, and next thing after that it's the morning. Place smells like home. Bacon and eggs and coffee. Table's all set. I was just finishin' my juice when I remembers about the fin. I go back into the bedroom and there's my clothes all washed and laid out. No five dollar bill. I check all the pockets. Nothin'. I goes out to the kitchen.

' "Breakfast's ready," says Dolly. She's got the plate in her hands.

' "Where the five dollar bill?"

' "What five dollar bill?"

' "You know damned well what five dollar bill."

' "I don't know what you're talkin' about."

'I gave her a little bat on the side of the head. Plate went flyin'. It was my last five. After that's gone, I got nothin', see. Now I'm callin' her names and then I go an' get my clothes on and I'm puttin' on my shoes and there's the five dollar bill, stuffed into the toe of my shoe. Musta put it in there when I took my pants off. For safe-keeping.'

His cigarette was right down to his fingertips. He took another half-drag and dropped it into the ashtray. He used another butt to stamp it out. He scratched his cheek. 'I went out and says "Sorry, sweetheart." But she's mad, see. She says "All them times you come in here drunk'n hungry." She says "All them times you lifted ten or twenty outta my purse thinkin' I never noticed." She says "All them times I'd come in the middle of the night and bring you home with me." She says "Get out." ' He looked up at me. Gave a kind of half-shake of his head. 'Never saw her again.' He looked right at me.

'I regret that.'

He got up. He came over by where I was sitting and grabbed his shirt off the floor. 'But that's it. My only regret. Money? Medals? What's that, eh?' He tucked his shirt in. He went looking for his shoes. One of them was under the bed. You could see the toe of it. The other one he had to search for. It took him a couple of minutes. It was over by the rad. He fingered back the curtain. Took a look at the day. 'Not a bad lookin' day out there.'

I was on my feet. Al was back on the bed. He had one shoe tied up. He was working on the other. He looked up. 'Sometimes I look back and think it all looks tragic.' He finished lacing his shoe and stood up. 'But sometimes it just seems funny. Life is how you see it, eh? But what's life? Three score and ten. Somethin' like that. Shit. Another ten years, I'll be gone.'

We were out in the hall. He shut his door. He hadn't locked it. I mentioned it to him. He turned and gave me one of those smiles. 'Ain't a whole lot worth stealin' in there, pal.' He laughed. Made for the stairs.

When we got out front he looked to his right, then to his left. 'Nice day to go down by the river.'

'Yes,' I said. 'That it is.'

'Be seein' ya,' he said.

'Yes,' I said.

'Say,' he said. 'Ain't got a fin you can make the loan of, have ya?'

*   *   *

IT WAS A MONTH OR MORE BEFORE I GOT BACK TO TOM REAUME'S PLACE.

Same big smile. Same offer of a coffee.

'I looked everywhere,' he said.

No snapshots. 'Just the ones up here.' He tapped his temple, as he'd done the last time.

'Maybe I could have a look at them,' I said.

He laughed. 'Well, let's see.'

'Tell me some of the things you remember as a kid.'

The snapsots came out. And like the real thing, they were in no particular order. Tom's mind was a kind of messy box.

Remembered Snapshots #1

The Westwood dance floor is crowded. One of those slow-moving mirrored balls suspended from the ceiling sprays starlight on the dancers. A lot of dreamy looks. In the background, a four-piece orchestra on a cramped stage.

Remembered Snapshot #2

That's Tom, as a boy, standing on the driver's seat of the cigar boat, one of those knifey-nosed mahogany beauties that crossed and recrossed the Detroit River all through Prohibition—like the one Dick Trout still owns—and turned a lot of people, including Tom's grandfather, into rich men. In this photo, Tom is wearing a large grin. So are the young cloth-capped men who will soon lift him back onto the dock and resume the loading: Burlap sacks filled with bottles of Canadian Club whisky.

Remembered Snapshot #3

Two men stand on the front porch of The Chappell House Tavern (later The Lido, later Rumrunners, long gone now). They're wearing baggy trousers. Their shirt sleeves are puffed out just below the bicep garters. Their cloth caps are tilted at a rakish angle. They're smirking.

The one on the left is Earl Reaume.

The one on the right is Les Trumble.

Les Trumble was a babe in his mother's arms the night his father, Babe, was gunned down inside The Chappell House by the Rev. J.O.L. Spracklin, holier-than-thou Methodist preacher, provincial liquor inspector, tub-thumping uplifter.

Spracklin later claimed Babe had a gun, although no guns other than those carried by Spracklin and his gang were ever found. Spracklin was acquitted. Of course.

Les Trumble took over the operation of the tavern when he was old enough to do so, which made him a competitor of Tom's dad, Ernest Earl, who had taken over the Brighton Beach Hotel from his dad when Albert John died. Standing on the front steps of Les Trumble's establishment, you could see Ernest Earl's establishment in the distance.

'There was always rivalry.

'Sometimes it was friendly.

'Sometimes not.'

The Brighton Beach, The Chappell House, The Dominion House, The Sunnyside, Thomas's Inn: These were the names of the legendary roadhouses of the southwest—all of them built at or before the turn of the twentieth century, all of them making vaults of money during the dry days of Prohibition.

None ever shut a day.

Remembered Snapshot #4

Tom and three pals are standing around a bonfire. There is a canvas tent near the edge of the clearing and beside it, a path, and in the distance you can just make out the river. The boys are standing to the left of the tent. Tom's the one on the left, fishing rod in his left hand, forefinger of his right hooked through the gills of a fish.

Smug little smile.

'In the summer, this is the early to mid-30s we're talking about, me and my pals used to pack up and leave home for a week or more at a time, pitching our tents in the bush down by the river.' Right about where the J. Clark Keith power plant was built, on the shore behind his father's hotel.

'We'd go down the bank to the gravel beach and walk along to the cement wharf.' Drop their lines in, hoping for the best. They didn't have to hope in the fields. They simply had to forage: Potatoes, tomatoes, corn, onions and whatever else they could find. Being careful not to get caught. 'Then we'd go back to the camp and cook ourselves a farmhand's supper.'

Remembered Snapshot #5

This one was taken on Hallowe'en Night, 1951, the night they moved into the house in which they still live. 'There wasn't even a road here. It was just a cow path. And there were only three or four houses between Seven Mile Road and Sandwich Street.'

Remembered Snapshot #6

In the background, Zug Island and the river. In the foreground, a shirtless crew hammering boards onto the skeleton of what will be one of the little cottages which face the river. If you look closely, you will see this is the same field as the one in which Tom and his pals, years before, had erected their tents and camped out.

'That's about it for snapshots.'

I thanked him.

'Not sure it was very helpful.'

You have no idea.

'One last question?'

'Shoot.'

'Know anything about blind pigs?'

'You're sitting in one. But I got nailed. Then I quit selling.'

*   *   *

YORKY HAD BEEN OUT OF SIGHT FOR QUITE A WHILE. OUT OF SIGHT, OUT OF mind. Then one day in court I ran into Anthony Quiller. He told me he'd heard Yorky was in a nursing home. I did a little snooping and sure enough. Even smaller, it seemed, than I remembered him. He was sitting in an armchair beside his bed. He smiled when I walked in.

'Hi Yorky.'

'Hello,' he said. Despite the smile, it was obvious he didn't remember me.

I told him my name. Told him I'd seen him around town. That I'd covered a few of his appearances in court.

'Oh,' he said. 'Yes. I had a few of those.' He laughed. Coughed. Laughed again. 'Oh, quite a few.'

I asked him if he'd mind talking to me for a while. Telling me his story. I told him I thought a lot of people would be interested to hear his story. He smiled.

'Oh, we used to booze it up all right. We used to sleep all over. We'd sleep anywhere. Under bushes. Or in cars in the winter. They used to call us winos. Sometimes we'd be locked up every night. Pay your fine the next day and away you'd go.'

I told him I'd heard he'd had about 700 convictions.

'There were never any dry spells.' Big laugh.

150

I asked him about his past.

'I was born in England,' he said. 'My Dad, he owned a glue factory. He was a chemist. We lived pretty well. I certainly lived it up.'

Yorky Story: One day, down by the side door of the Prince Edward Hotel, three policemen were struggling a diminutive drunk into the back of a paddy wagon.

An elderly woman happened by and, thinking the constables might hurt the tiny gray-haired man, muttered something about police brutality.

The little drunk stopped struggling, glowered and snapped: 'Mind your own business you silly old bitch,' and resumed his spreadeagled stance at the back door of the paddy wagon while the officers tried to get his hands free and shove him inside.

Then there was the time Yorky was sharing a jug with some friends.

Oh no you can't.

Oh yes I can.

And Yorky took the jug and headed in the direction of the CKLW TV tower, Riverside and Crawford. With two bucks hanging in the balance Yorky tackled the tower and got within about 100 feet of the top.

There wasn't any hurry, of course. Time for a nip and a couple of insults for the now-believing cronies way down there and the fire fighter clammering up to bring him down. No harm in doing a little loop-de-loop around one of the guy wires (so there would be absolutely no doubt about such matters later on).

The two dollars all but in his pocket, down he came at his own speed, basking in the admiration and awe of those on the ground. Cops and firefighters shaking their heads.

Trousers can be so troublesome. And so a blemish appeared on Norman Haworth's record of being drunk in a public place.

Indecent exposure, indeed.

'You were married?'

'My wife's name was Margaret.'

'You have a daughter?'

'Margaret. One daughter. I think one died. I'm not sure now. It's such a long time ago.

'I went to England five times. On boats. Got drunk on the boat. You could get booze on the boats. Boy, you got drunk. I was back five or six times. My father was a Grand Master in the Masons. He was a chemist.'

He leans back and coughs and falls silent.

Tired?

'Yes, I'm tired. I think I'd like to lie down.' He smiles and his eyes sparkle. 'You can't kill a good man.' And shadow-boxes. Right fist darting out. 'I can still hold my own. And if I can't win, I can run.' Laughter.

'Come back and see me.' He winks. 'And bring a bottle. It used to be Catawba.'

He folds in a fit of laughter and coughing.

*   *   *

THERE ARE DAYS WHEN YOU DON'T WANT TO BE OUT ON THE RIVER. TROUBLE is, that many of those days, like many marriages, start out beautifully. It's only later the storms move in. And some of the storms on the river—just like marriage break-ups—are breathtaking.

One evening, we were down at Lilly Kazilly's, the great little bar and marina right across from Peche Island. It was one of those enchanting evenings at the end of a hot and heavy-aired August day, when you're glad to be sitting on the patio at the river's edge, catching whatever breath of air might come wafting your way. So there we were, watching a couple of guys trolling out of either side of their very nice-looking eighteen-footer over near the Peche Island shore, when my friend Max said 'Would you look at that.'

I turned in my chair. From Lilly's patio you can see all the way down the river to the bridge, and down there, just beyond the bridge, the sky had turned a sickish grey-green and there was a wall of rain coming up the river. A moment later, you couldn't see the bridge. Then the skyline of Detroit disappeared. 'I think maybe we should watch this from inside,' said Max. The four of us grabbed our glasses and headed inside. The waitress was right behind with our plates. The other waitresses just had time to lower the umbrellas before the rain hit. And I do mean hit. Suddenly the sun disappeared and the sky was dark and it was like finding yourself inside a car wash, rain so heavy and hard against the glass that everything outside was distorted. Fifteen minutes later, our waitress was toweling off our table and chairs and we were back on the patio—temperature fifteen degrees cooler than it had been before the storm hit.

Like they say: If you don't like the weather, wait fifteen minutes.

Sometimes it's not a change for the best.

Roger Hunt remembers one day, he and Shelley Kidder were out in the backyard of their place in Brighton Beach. This was summer. 'The sky turned kind of purplish-green. I turned to Myrtle (Shelley's mother) and I told her "I'd like to see a tornado sometime." I'd no sooner said that than she pointed over my shoulder and there was a funnel cloud down at the river.'

Shelley Kidder: 'The sky was an awful green colour. And the air was awful still.'

Roger: 'And then the wind picked up and the rain started.'

Shelley: 'I grabbed our daughter and ran for the neighhour's. We don't have a basement, eh?'

Roger: 'I was trying to hurry Myrtle along, but by the time we got to the Arnold's, it was all over. I'll tell you this. I'll never wish for anything like that again.'

Shelley: 'Mrs. Arnold, she thought it was the end of the world. That's what she said.'

One of the worst tornados in Windsor's history made landfall in Brighton Beach. June 17, 1946. An F4. The tornado touched down across the river, behind Zug Island, then skipped across the river, ripped through Brighton Beach, then cut across what is now LaSalle. It cut through farmland and forest, narrowly missing the airport, seemed to lose some of its strength once it crossed Highway 3, but then touched down as an F4 again near Walker and Grand Marais, through Tecumseh before finally dissipating over Lake St. Clair.

The storm's path was roughly 100 feet wide and more than 30 miles long. The tornado knocked out power to most of the city for about a day, and damaged or destroyed roughly 400 homes in Windsor.

Seventeen people were killed.

*   *   *

YOU CAN ALWAYS TELL WHEN IT'S TIME TO WRITE AN OBIT. YORKY HAD BEEN on my mind ever since the nursing-home visit. Given his condition, I thought I'd better start doing the legwork. So I made the rounds—courthouse, police station, the Brock Street Jail—to piece together the fragments of his life.

First up, of course, Judge Gordon Stewart. We met in his office. He told me that he was looking out the window one day and there was Yorky, having difficulty walking. Luckily for him, he had one of Windsor's finest at each elbow. They almost got him inside the station house. 'He always seemed to be having trouble with his trousers.'

Judge Stewart had lots of favourite Yorky stories. For instance: On one occasion Yorky—wasn't charged with anything—just came in through the public-seating area, pushed through the swinging door and approached a very surprised Judge Stewart, whose court was in session. Yorky held up a bouquet of flowers. 'These are for you.'

Or the time he arrived in court through the usual door—the one leading in from the holding cells—and said he wanted to retain a lawyer. Stewart was a little startled—Yorky always pleaded guilty—but he put the matter over for a few days so Yorky could find one. The day arrived. Yorky arrived. No lawyer. 'I've changed my mind,' said Yorky. 'You can go ahead with the case.' The arresting officers gave their evidence. Stewart asked Yorky if he'd like to testify in his own defence. He respectfully declined. 'Convicted,' said Stewart. 'That'll be five days.'

'Say, your Majesty, I never did plead guilty.'

Stewart checked his notes. Conferred with the court clerk. Yorky was right. 'He hadn't pleaded. Case dismissed.'

There were lots of stories. Stewart remembered how, one Christmas, Yorky arrived with some cards, sat down at the judge's desk and wrote them out and handed one to him on the way out.

'You know, I never met anyone with a greater respect for the courts.' And he never heard of one of instance of Yorky stealing or being involved in any violence.

'I'll tell you this, a day without Yorky was a dull day. He was a class guy.'

Next up, Frank Montello. First thing I noticed in his office was a photo of Yorky, signed and framed, hanging on the wall.

Frank tried to get Yorky into the *Guinness Book of World Records*. He looked up Yorky's list of convictions. 'I got as far as about 700,' and then arrived at that point when accurate records were not kept, scuttling the project.

Yorky almost always came up before his pal Judge Stewart. But one day Stewart was sick and Yorky arrived in court to find himself facing Judge Thrasher. He leaned over to Frank and said, 'What do you know about this man?' and Frank said, 'Well, he's pretty fair.'

Judge Thrasher asked him how he pleaded, guilty or not guilty?

Yorky said 'Well, suppose I plead guilty, what would you do with me?'

It wasn't uncommon for Yorky to remind Stewart that his pension cheque—mailed to the Brock Street Jail—wouldn't be arriving for another seven days.

'I sentence you to seven days in jail.'

'Thanks, your Majesty.'

'One time he appeared after a few days away and said to Stewart "You gave me four days too much." There he'd been, pension cheque waiting for him, and he couldn't get out. Another time he complained "They let me out two days too soon. You should mind your arithmetic." He and Stewart were friends in a very real sense. They played to each other.'

Clients were waiting, so Frank saw me to the door.

'Are you going back to see him?'

I told him I was.

'Well, tell him that if he doesn't outlive us, he's got two pallbearers. Gord and I will be there.'

And, of course, I had to make my way to the Brock Street jail, where Jim Smith, Walt MacGuigan, and Bruce Bennett met me in the cluttered room just inside the main door.

Yorky stories? Oh yeah.

When Yorky was let out at the end of his frequent stays, the boys would slip him a dollar for bus fare downtown and a cup of coffee or a pack of smokes. And he'd always pay them back. He'd arrive and say, here, son, here's the dollar I owe you. And he'd insist they take it. Sometimes when it came to the end of his stay and it was snowing or raining or if his pension cheque hadn't arrived, he'd ask if he could stay an extra day or two.

'He kind of had the run of the place,' said Walt.

One time Yorky didn't feel like joining the work detail so he went up to see the jail doctor with a 'bad' back. The doctor said 'Sure, Yorky. No work.' And back down he came. 'And we found him walking in the corridor on his hands,' said Jim.

'He was the cock of the roost,' said Bruce. 'He policed the place. The others would listen to him, even the older, hardened ones. And the young people would come in and he'd tell them they were damned fools to spend their lives in a place like this.'

He had a sense of humour. 'One time,' said Jim, 'someone asked him what he did and, you know he was five feet tall and weighed maybe a hundred and ten soaking wet, and he smiled and said: "I'm the bouncer down at The Essex Hotel." '

One year, the jail's cook baked Yorky a birthday cake. 'That was the only party we ever had in here,' said Bruce.

'He came into some money form his family back in England,' said Jim. 'He went over to England to collect it. And when he got back he bailed out all his friends. That was the kind of guy he was.'

Finally, I visited Yorky's daughter, Margaret. 'I don't have many pictures of my dad,' she said. And she wondered if I could write the story without using her married name. 'All my friends know he's my dad. My enemies don't need to know.'

Of course.

'He came to Canada, to British Columbia, in 1920, to work in the mines. And then he sent for my mother, his girlfriend then. He'd left her money to come out after him. But she wouldn't come over if they weren't married. So he went back and married her. That was in Scotland. And then they came back to Windsor. He had a tinsmith's shop down on Caron Avenue near London Road (now University Avenue). He did eaves-troughing and tin-smithing and plumbing and furnace work. Masonry work. He worked all over.

'We lived in apartments. Lots of apartments. What we went through …

'He was born near Manchester. His dad had a glue factory and they were pretty well off. Not upper class, but upper-middle-class. His dad was a great friend of Charlie Chaplin.

'Dad had seven brothers and sisters. The last time I went up to see him he asked me "Are all my brothers dead?" I think two are still alive.' And each time a brother died, or another relative, some of the family money would find its way to Windsor.

'The last time, oh it wasn't a fortune, but it was a good bit of money. I got him all dressed up and sent him off on the boat. He had been living with my hubby and me on the farm. Oh, it was good out there. We would go hunting, he and I. And walking. And every once in a while my hubby would bring him a bottle of wine. And that was it. And it was like that until the money came. Off he went, just like that.

'Oh, I promised him everything if he'd quit drinking. You don't know all the things we tried. I'd say, we could take the children out for a picnic. But, no, he didn't want to go on picnics.

'It got so that family didn't matter anymore.

'Every now and then he'd phone, and he'd be crying, and I'd go down and bail him out. Or he'd show up at the door. I'd always have clean clothes for him. I'd keep them there. And he'd change and say, "Do you think you could make me a sandwich?" and I'd say "Sure, Dad, I'll make you a sandwich." And I'd make him two.

'And you know, he'd have left a friend up at the corner.

'Often I'd take things from my children—spend money on him. I'd buy him nice wool socks. And the next time I'd see him, he be wearing thin cotton socks again. He'd have sold the wool ones.

'What could I do? I had a family.

'My hubby, he'd say "He can stay if he's sober, but not if he's drunk." And he was right of course. I'd turn dad away and watch him walk away and oh, I'd cry and cry.

'My mum and dad split up in the 1940s. They'd still have been together if it wasn't for the drinking. She never stopped loving him.'

His wife Margaret died in 1966.

'What kind of Dad was he?'

'What we went through, you'll never know. God said respect your mother and father, but then again, I look at some of the things he's done and you weigh that. But I still love him. There was always a bond. It was a strange thing. "Phone me when you're sober Dad." He was always my Dad.

'I remember my dad taking me fishing and teaching me to fix furnaces. I was a good little furnace-fixer when I was a girl.

'I remember him running backwards with his hands in the pockets of his coat, his arms stretched out wide so I wouldn't have the winter wind in my face.'

*   *   *

AND THEN, SURE ENOUGH.

The front page of *The Windsor Star* Friday, November 30, 1984:

YORKY GETS CALL FROM HIGHER COURT

Beneath the headline, my byline.

Norman 'Yorky' Haworth, a little man with a large legend, was buried today.

Weren't many of us at the funeral home.

Margaret and a few other relatives. A couple of Yorky's drinking pals. There were four nice floral tributes, three from family and one—a couple of dozen white and red carnations—from Judge Stewart.

The judge was in the front row beside Frank Montello. I sat beside Frank.

As we drove to the cemetery in Montello's car, he and Stewart swapped stories.

'Remember the time he asked for a remand?' Montello asked. 'He told you he needed to get a new lens in his glasses.' Stewart nodded.

'Well, Gord and I were having a drink later in the bar of the old Prince Edward Hotel. Remember Gord? And there was a washroom right around the corner from the bar and I went in and there was Yorky. "I thought you had get a new lens in your glasses." Yorky had flashed one of his famous impish grins. 'He said "I didn't really need to. That's my bad eye anyway." And who should walk in right at that moment?'

Stewart laughed at the memory.

'We won't see too many like him in our lifetime,' said Stewart. 'Yorky never hurt anyone in his life. He was made for the courts. By that I mean he broke the routine. I guess he could be quite a drunk, but in the court he was the epitome of respect. And he could say things—he had a real wit—that would just break up the court.'

'He was a gentleman,' said Frank. 'He had the utmost respect for the court. He always conducted himself like a gentleman—unless someone tried to take his favourite seat in the prisoner's dock.'

'What's that cliché about "My Favourite Character?" ' asked Stewart. 'Well, I'm not saying goodbye to my favourite character. I'm saying goodbye to one of my favourite friends.'

When we got to the cemetery, Frank stopped his car behind the hearse. We got out and waited while the driver and his helper opened the back door and started to pull the coffin out. Judge Stewart took the front left, Frank the front right. A couple of guys I didn't know took the middle. The driver took the back left. He looked at me.

'Get that corner?'

'Yeah. Sure.'

So I got to be one of Yorky's pallbearers as well.

Did my best not to smile.

*   *   *

LOTS OF LITTLE REMNANTS OF HISTORY HERE AND THERE.

Drive out Sandwich Street to Highway 18, follow the turn where it becomes Front Road and you're in LaSalle, which is named, of course, for René-Robert Cavelier, Sieur de La Salle, who passed this way in 1679 or thereabouts, and whose influence is still felt: Lots of French-sounding names and Catholic churches in the oldest French settlement in Southwestern Ontario.

Who better to take you on an historic tour downriver?

Geoffrey pulled the old Cadillac to the curb in front of *The Star*. Opened the door. Mrs. Major welcomed me with a smile. Patted the seat beside her.

'I have something for you,' she said. 'You can read it on the way. It'll give you a sense of what we're driving into.'

She handed me an old book. Really old. It had a red leather cover and the edges of the pages were gold. It had a little cloth bookmark sewn into the binding.

'*The Diaries of Antoine Laumet dit de Lamothe Cadillac,*' she said. 'I was looking for something by LaSalle, but this will have to do.'

So this is what the Detroit River looked like, circa 1701.

The banks (of the Detroit) are so many vast meadows where the freshness of these beautiful streams keep the grass always green. These same meadows are fringed with long and broad avenues of fruit trees which have never felt the careful hand of the watchful gardener; and fruit trees, young and old, droop under the weight and multitude of their fruit and bend the branches toward the fertile soil which has produced them. In this soil so fertile, the ambitious vine which has not yet wept under the knife of the industrious vine-dresser, forms a thick roof with its broad leaves and heavy clusters.

Under these vast avenues you may see assembling in the hundreds shy stag and the timid hind with the bounding roe-buck, to pick eagerly of the apples and plums with which the ground is paved. The golden pheasant, the quail, the partridge, the woodcock, the teeming turtle dove, swarm in the wood and cover the open country intersected and broken by groves of full-grown forest trees. The woods are of six kinds—walnut trees, white oaks, red, bastard ash, ivy, white wood trees and cottonwood trees straight as arrows without knots of enormous size and height. It is from thence the fearless eagle looks steadily at the sun.

The fish there are fed and laved in sparkling and pellucid waters and are nonetheless delicious for the beautiful supply. There are such large numbers of swans that the rushes among which they are massed might be mistaken for lilies. The gabbling goose, the duck, the teal and the bustard are so common there that they move aside to allow a boat to pass.

In a word, the climate is temperate, the air very pure; during the day there is a gentle wind and at night the sky, which is always placid, diffuses sweet and cool influences which cause us to enjoy the benignity of tranquil sleep.

'Pellucid waters,' I said.

'Exactly,' she said.

We'd taken the turn at the end of Sandwich—we could see the old Brighton Beach Hotel off to our right—then another turn onto old Highway 18 past the raceway, and another turn onto Old Front Road. And there we were in LaSalle.

The Chateau was on our right. The Sunnyside up ahead.

'All these old roadhouses were very colourful,' said Mrs. Major.

'Ever frequent them?' I asked.

She gave me a look best described as mortified. 'Me?'

'Just wondering.'

'This is another book you should read,' she said. She pulled a copy of *The Township of Sandwich* from the crocheted cloth bag at her feet. 'It's by Frederick Neal. A little on the dry side. But filled with useful information. Now that you're so keen on local history, you should get a copy. Perhaps they have a copy in the library at *The Star*.'

We were on the far side of LaSalle now, heading for Amherstburg. 'Pull over here, Geoffrey.' Geoffrey brought us to a graceful halt on the gravel shoulder just this side of a bridge.

'This,' said Mrs. Major, 'is a very important site.' She seemed to say 'very' in italics.

'Geoffrey.'

Geoffrey got out, came around the back and opened the door. Held out his hand and helped Mrs. Major to disembark. Then offered to help me as well. I waved him off. 'Thanks, though.'

Mrs. Major was marching—no other way to describe it—down the gravel shoulder in her high heels. She stopped at the approach to the bridge, turned to see where I was. 'Come along,' she said. It was like I was back in school, on a field trip.

'I'll just read you a little passage,' she said. Her glasses were hanging from a little gold cord. She placed them on her nose and opened Neal's book, held it out at a distance and began to recite. She had a very nice voice. A little on the plummy side, but nice.

'General Hull and his whole force started down the military road against Fort Malden. Colonel Proctor, who was in command at Malden, nothing daunted, advanced with a force of about 400 regulars, militiamen and Indians to the Canard River and there taking up a position on the lower side of the marsh awaited for the Americans to attempt the crossing.'

Mrs. Major lowered her glasses. Raised her right arm, pointing across the bridge. 'Right over there,' she said. 'That's where they waited.' She replaced her glasses, began again to read:

> In silence they waited as the column reached the bridge. A volley thundered from the reeds on the further side. The American force was staggered, and under the deadly rain of volley after volley broke into disorderly retreat.

> They retired beyond Turkey Creek and rallied near the present site of Chappell's hostelry.

> Major Semandre of the militia followed the invaders beyond the creek and then, carefully concealing his followers with a band of Tecumseh's braves, he walked on almost to the American camp. Drawing his pistol he fired at point blank range into the throng of soldiers and dashed away with a large number in pursuit. He led them right into the muzzles of the muskets of his men when a volley was poured into the pursuers. Half of them were laid low and the balance withdrew in confusion to their camp.

> After this reception, Hull gave up any idea of attacking Malden and withdrew and on learning General Brock had arrived in Malden with reinforcements, General Hull recrossed to Detroit on August 7 and retreated to Home Ground.

Mrs. Major removed her glasses. Closed the book. 'Thrilling, isn't it? To be standing where all this transpired so many years ago.'

What else could you say? 'Yes,' I said.

'Geoffrey.' Geoffrey, who had been standing with us, turned and trotted back to fetch the Caddy.

'Where to, ma'am?'

'Back to town,' said Mrs. Major. 'That will do for today. Perhaps next week we'll go to Amherstburg. It's a treasure,' she said.

Geoffrey pulled a U-turn and we headed back through LaSalle.

Back then, in the mid-60s, LaSalle was a place you drove through on your way downriver to Amherstburg and then back. You could stop at the Chateau or the Sunnyside for a burger and a beer. There were some marinas and boatyards, a gas station or two. Oddly enough, considering that LaSalle was built right beside the river, you couldn't more than catch a glimpse of it now and then, Front Road being a fair bit inland.

'During Prohibition, this was quite an active spot,' said Mrs. Major. 'All kinds of canals down there.' She pointed out the left-side windows, her extended finger right in front of my nose. 'And boathouses, of course. Filled with whisky. The bootleggers brought their boats in under the cover of darkness. Loaded them with whisky and ran over to the other shore.'

I thought of Dick Trout, down at the end of one of these lanes.

'Why are you smiling,' said Mrs. Major.

'Just thinking of all that whisky,' I said.

'A lot of local men became very rich,' she said. 'As they say, a lot of Windsor's finest homes were built of bottles.

'And, of course, the roadhouses did a thriving business. Some ladies became quite wealthy as well.'

'Ladies?' I said.

'Of the nocturnal variety,' she said.

'Oh,' I said.

These days LaSalle isn't quite that exciting. It's become a thriving bedroom town, right next door to Windsor: Lots of very expensive new homes, lots of trails through big swaths of trees that developers probably would have preferred to cut down but which town officials have gone to great lengths to save.

Like most little towns, this one claims some pretty famous daughters and sons: Olympic swimmer Amanda Reason, NFLer Luke Wilson, former NHLers Andy Delmore and Derek Wilkinson, one-time Washington Senators pitcher Pete Craig, DJ Richie Hawtin. Members of the rock band the Tea Party—Jeff Martin, Jeff Burrows and Stuart Chatwood—all grew up in LaSalle.

My favourite LaSalle famous son is Bill Stidworthy. He would not have considered himself famous. And he wasn't exactly a native son, having been born in Britain, but he lived in a neat little house on a canal in LaSalle. Bill was an artist. Worked in watercolours, mostly. Landscapes. Simple. Evocative.

I learned about him when Ken Saltmarche wrote a review of one of his shows for *The Star*. Ken was an artist, and at the time was director of the Art Gallery of Windsor. This is part of what he wrote: 'Walking into Bill Stidworthy's exhibit is a bit like flopping down in a field on a sunny day and listening to the bird songs, smelling the grass, or watching the clouds roll by. It is frankly nostalgic (I expect some of my sophisticated friends would call it "camp"), and I, for one, like it.'

So off I went to see the show. Great stuff.

'Hi. Mr. Stidworthy. I wonder if I …'

'Well, of course.' And he gave me the directions to his charming little house/studio, which sat on the banks of a canal cut in from the Detroit River, beside tree-shaded, dusty graveled Martin Lane. Artist's palette out front for a name sign. Martin Lane, long since paved, looks nothing now like it did when I first pulled up in front of Bill's frame cottage one August day in 1974. It's all lookalike cookie-cutter very-expensive raised ranches now. Back then, every house was just like every resident: One-of-a-kind and a little off-kilter. Bill fit right in.

He was 85 when I met him—had three more years to go.

He had a face which I once described as rugged and leathery. I'm looking at his photograph as I write this and rugged/leathery doesn't quite do it justice. Chiselled, I'd say, deeply lined and creased. A lot of miles on that face. But the word I'd choose today is 'kindly.' A thatch of white hair combed straight back with his hands.

Bill and I headed out back to sit on the dock by the little canal—the dock where he held his classes for more students than he could remember—so we could have a little chat. I thought we'd be chatting about his painting, but he wanted to talk about the floods which, a year before, had disrupted his life, almost destroyed the house. He pointed out the high-water marks and the damage the floods had done to his property and his neighbours', forcing them all to flee. We went back inside and he gave me a tour of the place, showing me where things had been destroyed by the water and then repaired and repainted once the waters had receded. 'Aggravating,' he said. But then went right on to talk about all his friends and neighbours who showed up to help clear away the wreckage, cart damaged stuff off to the dump, then come back en masse to help clean the place up, paint it and move Bill and his wife back into their home. 'I'll never forget that.'

He shuffled out of the studio and into the living room, pointing at different paintings, telling a little about the history of each. Pictures painted from the Gaspe to Vancouver Island at one time or another in his long, long career. He stopped before a huge oil hanging over the fireplace. 'Those are the islands where the boys used to go hunting.' He focussed for a second or two, as though going through that painting into a time long lost. 'I didn't do that many oils. I'm a watercolour man.' And there were watercolours of the foothills of Alberta, the meadows of Haliburton, the forests and mountains of British Columbia and: 'This one, I did just down the road. I don't go far to paint anymore.'

There was another mountain scene—he worked for the railroad for a time painting crossing signs through the mountains—and a little meadows watercolour-sketch from a rack at the back of his worktable, a sketch he did while studying under Carl Schaefer. 'He liked my sketches.' Then a sketch, done from a newspaper picture, of the cabin Tom Thomson used as a studio in Toronto. 'We missed a man when we missed him.' He put them back in their place in a storage rack. He walked to his workbench, cluttered with half-done sketches, paint pots and brushes, odds and ends. 'I don't keep my stuff properly. I'm a very disorderly man.'

Standing there by his workbench, Bill Stidworthy spoke of the future. 'I think we'll be the foremost country in the world in art some day,' he said, looking out toward the canal. 'I won't be here, of course.' And I was reminded of what he'd said earlier, while we were out on the dock, looking around at the place he loved. 'I've had a very, very nice life.' And then, in the studio, he was saying so again, in different ways. Bringing up little fragments of that life: Attending art school in his native Torquay; spending Saturday afternoons with his grandfather in the galleries of London; the jobs painting in the hotels of the west when there wasn't any other work he could find, a job which nearly ended his life. He'd tumbled from a scaffold while painting a hotel ceiling in Victoria, smashing his left arm. 'It's still wired up and doesn't work properly.'

He recalled evenings spent in the foothills of the Rockies, sketching. He'd sell those sketches for four or five dollars. 'Enough to buy a bottle and have a party. When I remember how we lived, it's surprising we ever got through it.' He recalled the cow-punching and fence-mending near the Medicine Hat area where later—married and a father—he'd tried his hand at farming and went broke. The long winters when Bill-the-Farmer had to go into the woods and peel bark from the trees to keep the wood stove going. The twelve long years he spent painting walls and ceilings in The Prince Edward Hotel in downtown Windsor, coming home exhausted at day's end and still wanting to paint. Pictures.

Wound up in his little place by the canal where he could paint to his heart's content. He'd been up since 8:30 that morning and worked through until I arrived at four in the afternoon, with only a half-hour's break for lunch.

Time running out.

The days of selling sketches for four or five bucks were behind him. Bill Stidworthy was selling his watercolours for $200 or $300 each. A princely sum for him. When he wasn't painting pictures, he was painting little get-well cards to send to friends, framing pictures he'd promised someone.

All in all, a fine life there by the canal.

'My father had a saying. "You've got to make someone happy each day." I try to live by that.'

He looked out the window, then turned his gaze upon me.

'I feel this way about life. I would like to leave it with a lot of friends.'

*   *   *

BRIGHTON BEACH. WASN'T ALL THAT FAR OUT OF MY WAY. JUST A QUICK drive-through.

Shirley Caza and her husband Robert were on my must-meet list.

As luck would have it, they were home.

Shirley and Robert moved to Brighton Beach in 1957. Two kids. Another on the way. 'I hated it,' she said. 'We moved here in March. Nothing to do. The bus stop so far away. I hated it.'

That was then. Now?

She couldn't see herself living anywhere else.

'The neighbours aren't on top of you, 'buzz buzz buzz.' It's great here in the summer. We've had great parties. The kids' friends had a band. The neighbours'd come over and join us. The police weren't called.

'It's not hot out here. Not like in the city where the heat stays on top of you. Three-quarters of the time there's a gorgeous breeze. It's like the country, in a way. Another thing: I'm a nature lover. I like it out in the bush. It's not too safe now, what with bush bikes, but it used to be beautiful.

'I seen a fawn. This was about three years ago. Someone got him. Poachers, eh? You hang around long enough, the squirrels'll be right up on that screen door. In 1957, it was just about the same. Maybe even quieter. There were pheasants in the fields.'

She knew what others think—those who live in the city.

'My granddaughter got in a cab to come down here. She gave the cabbie my address. The cabbie, he said he didn't know where that was. He called the dispatcher. The dispatcher, he says, "Oh, she wants to go down to dogpatch." "Oh," says the cabbie, "I know where that is. You know where that name came from? Anyone didn't want a dog, drive down to Brighton Beach, open the door, shove the dog out, drive off." '

Once there was a little store. Mrs. Hawchuk's Store. 'It was just a little store (Chappus and Sandwich), but it was great. The kids loved it. It was nice and clean. She had lunch meats, hot dogs, soups, butter. It wasn't a big store. There was an apartment in the back they rented out. They sold flour, bread, eggs. It was a little grocery. It was good for the neighbourhood. Good for the kids. They could get candy, ice cream and pop through the summer.

'Then Helen's husband Mike died.

'Another couple bought the store. They drank a lot and fought a lot. The place'd be open one day and the next day not.

'Finally it closed.'

Another neighbourhood feature, of course, was The Westwood.

'I remember going in to the Westwood for my first drink. You had to be twenty-one then. Way back then, one side was the Men's and the other side was Ladies and Escorts, and you couldn't go in that side without an escort.

'There was a floor to dance on. It used to have windows. And a porch. On the Sandwich-Street side.

'There was the odd fight, but never anything major, shootings or stabbings or that. Though you'd get your odd one now and then.

'But we used to have fun.'

Speaking of fun.

When asked how many Brighton Beach residents have gone out of their way down through the years to ensure their neighbours didn't drop dead of the thirst, Robert Caza began to count them off, tip of his right index finger against the tips of the fingers of his other hand.

'One, two, three, four, five.

'Chris, Marg, Garbula, Myrt, Ma Ouellette.'

Shirley Caza: 'Everyone knew Ma Ouellette.'

Robert Caza: 'They didn't bother nobody. And if they weren't sellin' beer, they'd of been on welfare.'

Shirley Caza: 'So, put it this way. No one ever died of the thirst in Brighton Beach.'

Lots of characters.

'Old Mister Marchand lived in one of those shacks down by the river. A lot of people used to fish down by the river. People would drive down there wanting to park in the field. Old Man Marchand would charge them a quarter to get in and park.

'Just like he owned the land.'

When the residents were told they had to leave, with or without their shacks, 'Mister Marchand he tied his shack to his tractor and dragged it down the road. He moved it onto Chappus. He lived there with a woman named Marg. She used to sing. She had a nice voice, except when she got polluted.

'They'd go off first thing in the morning. He'd be driving his tractor and she'd be on the flatbed trailer he was towing. She'd be singing, as often as not. Seven at night, they'd come back. Marg would be flat out on the trailer, arm dangling over the side.'

And then there were the LaForge brothers.

'The LaForge Brothers, Wilbert and I don't know what the other one was, you'd see them by the side of the road, sleeping it off.

'I remember one time Wilbert got it into his head to saw a branch off a tree. He got out onto that branch and commenced sawing. The boys were calling up to him: "You're sawing on the wrong side." But he waved them off.

'Kept on sawing.

'And down it come.

'And him on it.

'Oh,' she said. 'I'll miss this place.

'A lot of the kids who grew up here, moved back here and raised their kids. They'll all be scattered, eh?'

*   *   *

A FEW DAYS AFTER I'D INTERVIEWED BILL STIDWORTHY, HE CALLED TO SAY thanks for the article. 'Do you think you could drop by?'

A couple of hours later I pulled in at his drive. He waved from his window, met me at the door.

'I've got a little something for you,' he said. 'Come here.' He led me into his studio.

When we'd talked a few days earlier, Bill had mentioned the art school he'd attended in England. I told him I'd been to Torquay, and he gave me an odd look, as though he didn't quite believe me or thought I was being condescending. We were flipping through photographs of Devon. He turned the page. I put my finger on the photo.

'Cockington Forge,' I said. The photograph showed a thatch-roofed forge—once a working forge, now a tourist destination. 'People write their names on scraps of paper, fold them up and stick them in the thatch.'

Bill had looked at me. 'You *were* there.' And then just a flash of embarrassment, having let me know he hadn't believed me when I told him I'd been to Torquay.

'Here,' he said. 'This is for you.'

A painting of the forge—all greenery and sunshine—a picture I treasure.

'You didn't have to do this,' I said.

'Yes I did.'

*   *   *

THERE ARE 28 ISLANDS IN THE DETROIT RIVER. SIX OF THEM ARE OURS. The loveliest of these is Peche Isle (or Peach Island to most people), a tiny wooded gem which you'll encounter almost as soon as you sail into the river from Lake St. Clair. Peche is 86 acres, has some lovely inlets and lagoons, the remains of some of the attempts to turn it into a mid-river resort or getaway, and some beautiful beaches.

Thanks to Henry Shanfield, there will be no more grand plans for golf courses or ski hills (no kidding), because thanks to Henry, Peche Isle is now a City of Windsor Park.

Oh, Henry.

Lots of people thought Henry was a bit loopy. He was skinny and gawky, had sparse grey hair which tended to fly around when he rode his old-fashioned white-walled no-speeds bike around town. This was long before bikes were fashionable for anybody but kids. People would just sort of think: 'There goes Henry,' and more-or-less dismiss him and his fanatical campaign to get the province, get the city, get *anyone* to buy Peche Island and turn it into a park.

Guess who had the last laugh?

Henry wasn't the loopy one.

The really loopy ones were those who had grand plans for a tiny island: Plans which, had they come to fruition, would probably have caused Peche Island to sink below the river's surface. Golf courses? Hotels? Ski hills? Seriously?

The island has had a series of owners—including Hiram Walker—all of whom came up with grand schemes. Hiram built a big house at the head of the island—40 or so rooms, according to some reports—and later owners thought they might turn the mansion into a resort hotel.

A fellow named Manny Harris came up with a truly loopy plan. Manny leased a couple of boats—I seem to remember them being about 60 or 70 feet long—loaded them with booze and journalists (one boat left from Windsor, the other from Detroit) and took us up the river to his little island, where we were treated to a big presentation about his plans.

He was apparently hoping that after enough drinks, we'd think his plan was brilliant and write stories saying as much. Then the politicians, whose help he needed (some of whom were along for the drinks and the ride) would give him whatever approvals were necessary to turn his plan into reality.

Well, good luck with that. Not even God could have turned his plan into reality.

Manny was going to fill in the lagoons and turn the place into a resort with a golf course and hotels. We watched and listened and took notes, then we got back on his boats and drank our way down the river to our respective docks—Canadian and American. Despite all the booze, or because of it, we thought this was the craziest scheme anyone had yet come up with for that 86-acre island. The general consensus was that Manny's grand plan would never see the light of day. We were right.

Conspicuous by his absence on that little free-for-all was Henry Shanfield.

In 1971, due to lobbying by Henry and his pals, the province bought the island with the intention of having it used as a kind of outdoor classroom where local students could learn about the flora and fauna of the area. Provincial bureaucrats came up with some grand schemes of their own: A million dollars worth of improvements—nature trails, picnic shelters, washrooms and so forth—but the plans went nowhere, the province pleading poverty. In 1974, the property was designated a provincial park for administrative and budget purposes, but the designation was really an empty promise. There was one employee and no funds to develop or even maintain the island.

Finally the City of Windsor bought the island for use as a municipal park.

So there it sits, woods and beaches and lagoons, much as it must have appeared when the natives first used it as a base for their fishing operations: Thus the name (which means 'fish', not 'peach').

Henry Shanfield lived long enough to see it. How do you spell vindication?

Just downstream, at the end of Bill Stidworthy's and Dick Trout's canals, is Fighting Island. It's uninhabited, but humans are hoping to turn it into a wildlife sanctuary in the midst of one of the most heavily-industrialized parts of North America.

There's been a successful lake sturgeon program, in which artificial spawning grounds were constructed on a one-acre site adjacent to the island. But that's just a tiny bit of what's been happening.

The island is part of LaSalle, but is owned by BASF Corporation which, along with its predecessors, used the island as a dump for alkaline by-products from the manufacture of soda ash and other lime-based products created at its facilities on the U.S. shore. The beds, used between 1924 and 1982, hold about 20 million cubic meters of calcium chloride, sodium chloride, coke ashes, un-reacted limestone, and limestone impurities such as silica, alumina, and metallic oxides. Handy. But not healthy. And then someone at BASF saw the light. In the mid-1970s, BASF brass decided to bring the island back to life. The company rebuilt the perimeter containment dikes, started an intensive re-vegetation program and set goals to reduce dust problems, increase wildlife habitat, control run-off and just make the island look beautiful once more.

The company has gone to great lengths to improve the quality of the soil on the island. It has created drainage systems and applied great quantities of compost in order to make the soil suitable for trees, shrubs and other plants. It has planted nearly six miles of windbreaks and more than 45,000 trees. It has acquired and applied organic biosolids to improve the quality of the soil in what were once lime beds. The result of all these efforts? Vegetative cover has increase from 40% of the southern three-quarters of the island to 80%. The birds have come back, dust complaints from mainland neighbours have decreased and the island is looking like an island once more: All trees, shrubs and songbirds.

The other Canadian islands in the stream:

Crystal Island: An uninhabited 92-acre, long, skinny island just above Boblo. The island was a dumping ground for millions of cubic yards of sediment dredged from the Detroit River's shipping lanes. The island's main attraction is Crystal Bay, where swift river currents flush out the pollution and keep the waters unusually clear. Thus the island's name.

Turkey Island: 39 acres, just off the southeastern tip of Fighting Island. Densely wooded and (except for partying teenagers) uninhabited.

Grass Island: Like Crystal Island, but half its size, this one is also long and narrow. It's located between Fighting Island and the Canadian shore. Well wooded, but (except by partying teenagers) uninhabited.

Not to be confused with Grassy Island, which is the name of the island on the opposite and American side of Fighting Island.

And way downriver, of course, Boblo, which, from 1898 until 1993, was an amusement park. Kids came to Boblo for the rides: The Nightmare, Falling Star, Wild Mouse, Sky Streak, and Screamer. There was a ferris wheel and a zoo, and to get from once place to another there was a little railroad. There was a huge dance hall—said to be the second-largest in the world—financed by Henry Ford, which could hold as many as 5,000 dancers.

There were a couple of beautiful steamboats—*SS Ste. Clair* and *SS Columbia* (the 'Boblo Boats')—which could each take 2,500 people the 18 miles from Detroit downriver to the island. A sight to see.

Splendid, while it lasted. But like Crystal Beach in Fort Erie and Sunnyside in Toronto, along with dozens of others in Canada and the United States, Boblo's time passed. The rides have long since been dismantled.

Boblo is now all houses and condos. Homeowners take a little ferry back and forth to Amherstburg. The big steamboats? A non-profit group was given the *SS Columbia,* which it is restoring for use as a sort of floating heritage museum on the Hudson River in New York. A volunteer group in Detroit is hoping to do the same with the *SS Ste Claire.*

Love to tell you more. But I was never on the boats or on the island.

*   *   *

'HEY, HEMINGWAY.' THE CITY EDITOR HELD HIS HAND OVER THE TELEPHONE mouthpiece. 'Line three. It's your girlfriend.'

Go ahead, laugh.

Mrs. Major said that she and Geoffrey would be by about two o'clock to pick me up, if that was suitable.

'Where are we going?'

'Amherstburg,' she said.

'Right.'

And right on the dot, Geoffrey pulled up in front of *The Star*, got out, opened the back door, then closed it after I'd settled in beside Mrs. Major.

The old Caddy purred down Riverside and through LaSalle and over the bridge where the Yanks were turned back by Colonel Proctor and his Indian allies. 'Turn right here, Geoffrey. Take us through the town, then back to the fort.'

'Right ma'am.'

'That's Boblo Island,' said Mrs. Major. 'Have you been there?' she wondered. 'No,' I said.

'Ghastly.' She seemed to shudder at the thought. 'All those children eating candy floss. Running around with their sticky fingers, touching things, and screaming. I can't imagine.'

'I'm with you there,' I said. 'Not a big fan of amusement parks.'

Apart from its proximity to the ghastly amusement park, Mrs. Major thought Amherstburg 'entirely charming.' Say this for Amherstburg: *Someone* somewhere along the line saw the wisdom of *not* tearing down historic buildings.

We parked in front of Fort Malden.

Time for today's history lesson.

'Amherstburg is where it is because the British thought it an ideal place to build a fort,' said Mrs. Major. 'And they needed a fort to guard against invasions and incursions and other rudeness perpetrated by all those cheeky Americans just over there on the other side of Bois Blanc Island.'

It was because of those Americans that the fort was built on what is now the Canadian shore. 'The British had originally built Fort Detroit, but had to cede the fort and other holdings in the U.S. as a result of The Jay Treaty, signed in 1796.

'Do you know about The Jay Treaty?' asked Mrs. Major.

I shook my head. 'Afraid not.'

'Well,' she said, 'read up on it some time. I think you'll find it illuminating.'

(Afraid to say I never got around to doing that.)

'So they—the British—crossed the river and built a new fort and named it Fort Amherstburg. They also constructed the King's Navy Yard so they could build ships which could travel and trade in the lakes above Niagara Falls.'

Then came The War of 1812, and there were all those pesky Americans again. 'U.S. General Hull, commander of Fort Detroit, had the gall to invade Canada in July of that year.'

Soldiers from Fort Amherstburg sent him and his troops packing. They won Fort Detroit, but lost the Battle of Lake Erie and were forced to give the fort back to the Americans again. Since they'd lost most of their canons—they were put on British ships to help fight the war out there on Lake Erie—the British decided to regroup in friendlier climes: They destroyed Fort Amherstburg and headed back east.

'The Americans came back down the river,' said Mrs. Major, 'built a new fort on the site and called it Fort Malden, which, when the war was over, was reclaimed by the British. But with no war to fight, they let the fort fall into disrepair. Such a shame.

'It was briefly brought back to life as a military installation to protect Upper Canada during the rebellion of 1837. But after that it was no longer of any use as a fort. It was abandoned by the military in 1851.

'It was turned into a lunatic asylum,' said Mrs. Major. 'The employees lived in one of the barracks buildings. The other two barracks were used to house the asylum's inmates—one for males, the other for females. The asylum was closed in 1870.'

'What then?' I said.

'There was a lumber mill on the property at one time. And then people starting building houses on the grounds.'

Someone saw the light. In 1937 the Canadian government bought the site and began bringing it back to life as the Fort Malden National Historic site.

'So,' said Mrs. Major.

'So?'

'Time to go home Geoffrey.'

'Right, ma'am.'

Right.

*   *   *

WHAT IS IT WITH ISLANDS AND WACKY PLANS?

Belle Isle is just downriver from Henry Shanfield's park. Belle Isle *is* a park—a little rundown these days given Detroit's precarious financial position—and a lovely one. At 900 and some odd acres, it's the largest urban island park in the United States. The island is listed on the National Register of Historic Places. It is home to the Anna Scripps Whitcomb Conservatory (1904), the Detroit Yacht Club, the Detroit Boat Club, the James Scott Memorial Fountain, and the Dossin Great Lakes Museum. There's also a Nature Centre which allows visitors to do something they'd have a hard time doing anywhere else in downtown Detroit: Walk wooded trails and look at natural habitats for wildlife. And, of course, there's a beach.

The latest nutty plan? A local developer said he and some backers would be willing to spend $1 billion to buy the island and turn it into a 'semi-independent city state' whose 35,000 citizens would cough up $300,000 each for the privilege of living there. They would have their own laws, government and currency. Drawings showed a clutch of high-rise buildings towering over what is now the memorial fountain, with housing extending to the eastern end of the island.

The plan died a timely death.

The island languishes, for now.

Now and then someone comes up with a really *bright* idea about islands.

Companies like BASF Corporation have worked wonders restoring places like Fighting Island. And cumulatively, all these efforts are paying off. Mayflies have returned to the Detroit River, which is an important sign of improved water quality. Lake whitefish are spawning in the Detroit River for the first time since 1916. Bald eagles are nesting and producing young in seven locations along the Detroit River. The Detroit River is a major waterfowl migration corridor. The River has one of the highest diversities of plants and animals in the Great Lakes Basin, and has been designated as a Biodiversity Investment Area by the United States and Canadian governments: 29 species of waterfowl are commonly found on the Detroit River and 65 species of fish are found in it. The Detroit River has an international reputation for its walleye fishery. It is estimated that walleye fishing alone brings in $1 million to the economy each spring.

Pretty impressive, given the way industries have historically treated the river. Long gone are Cadillac's 'sparkling and pellucid waters.' Beginning at the end of the 19th century, industry came to the shores of the Detroit River and the people running those industries seemed to believe that whatever they dumped in the river would just go away. Everyone got a big wake-up call in the 1940s. Historically, the lower part of the Detroit River froze from shore to shore in the winter. Once industries sprouted up and began discharging their effluents directly into the river, the water warmed and, come winter, there were open patches. The lower half of the river also features many islands and shoals and plentiful food for ducks, geese and swans. You can see where this is going. Given the plentiful food and large areas of open water, waterfowl began to spend the winter. Unbeknownst to the wildlife, these opened patches were coated with oil.

Oil and water don't mix. Neither do oil and ducks. Oil hampers a duck's ability to float. Coat their feathers and ducks can, and do, drown. Coat their feathers and ducks lose their insulation and can freeze to death. Coat their feathers and ducks can't fly or swim and will starve to death. Which brings us to the winter of 1948, when an estimated 11,000 ducks were killed by Detroit River oil polluion.

Hunters were outraged, and collected thousands of duck corpses and threw them on the lawn of the State Capitol building in Lansing. Hunters vote. And they got noticed. The following year, the Michigan Legislature established the Michigan Water Resources Commission. The definition of pollution was broadened and state approval was required for all new uses of state waters. Although shoreline industries were the biggest problem, there were many other sources of pollution: Municipal waste-water treatment plants, government installations, sewer overflows, and discharges of various kinds from ships. They were all targeted and between the late-1940s and the mid-1970s there was a 97% reduction in oil discharges into the Detroit River. Good news for the ducks. Winter kills decreased dramatically. Good news for politicians. No more dead ducks on the legislative lawns.

But there were more problems: In 1969 part of the oil-covered Rouge River caught fire. A few years later there was a 100,000-gallon oil spill in the Rouge, contaminating 27 miles of the lower Rouge and both shores of the Detroit River. The clean-up cost $7.5 million.

And yet. People on both sides of the river began talking about creating a wildlife refuge, and in 2000, Herb Grey, then the deputy prime minister, and John Dingell, a U.S. congressman, asked scientists and land-use managers to come up with a plan to protect and enhance the Detroit River ecosystem.

The result was *A Conservation Vision for the Lower Detroit River Ecosystem.* 'In ten years the lower Detroit River ecosystem will be an international conservation region where the health and diversity of wildlife and fish are sustained through protection of existing significant habitats and rehabilitation of degraded ones, and where the resulting ecological, recreational, economic, educational, and quality of life benefits are sustained for present and future generations.'

Lofty words. But for once, someone acted. The U.S. passed a law in 2001 creating the 410-acre Humbug Marsh as the centerpiece of The Detroit International Wildlife Refuge refuge. The marsh contains the last mile of natural shoreline along the U.S. side of the Detroit River. Lots of neat stuff in here: Shagbark hickories, oaks, ash and elm and dogwood, bulrushes, native and naturalized grasses, cat tail and the not-always-welcomed phragmites. Migratory songbirds love the marsh, and fish and waterfowl seem to as well.

The waters around Sugar Island, just off the southeast end of Grosse Ile and a mile from Boblo Island, are a haven for the endangered channel darter. The island has the only two sand beaches of any significance on the U.S. side of the river. Grassy Island, just north of Grosse Ile, is 72 acres now, but was a lot smaller before it became a dumping ground for millions of cubic yards of sediments and who knows what else dredged during the expansion of River Rouge. Although constructed of contaminated dredge material surrounded by dikes, fish don't seem to mind. At least 30 species—including rock bass, yellow perch, and emerald shiner—are spawning around the island. Despite all the stuff that was dumped on the island, the trees have come back: Eastern cottonwood, box elder, staghorn sumac, and willow. And where there are trees, there will be birds, lots of them, during spring and fall migrations.

Mud Island, the northernmost feature of the refuge is tiny—just 18 and a half acres. The island was donated to the refuge by National Steel Corporation in 2001. Three quarters of the island is forested— red maple, silver maple, white ash, cottonwood and willow—and, like Grassy Island, it's an important stopover for neotropical migrant birds during spring and fall. Warbling vireos can often be heard in the breeding season from the tops of the cottonwoods. The seventy or so acres of shallow shoals surrounding the island are just a couple of feet deep and support aquatic species such as wild celery. The Ecorse Channel, which separates the island from the U.S. mainland, is a popular fishing spot. It's also popular with dabbling ducks and swans— mute and tundra—which are commonly seen in great numbers taking advantage of all that wild celery.

Technically, there's a sixth island in the refuge. Except you can't see it. It's just east of the northern tip of Grosse Ile. Mamajuda Island is the smallest of all charted Islands in the Detroit River. Once upon a time it was about 30 acres, but much of it has been lost to erosion. Only a tiny portion of it, mostly boulders, is above the surface of the river, and that only occurs when river levels are low. Otherwise the whole thing is (barely) submerged and just a part of the much larger Mamajuda Shoal. The refuge, originally just 300 acres, has now grown to more than 5,700.

So, things can happen.

And you're wondering.

The proper name is The Detroit *International* Wildlife Refuge.

Windsor's Citizens Environment Alliance issued a press release in 2011 on the 10th anniversary of the creation of the refuge. Worth quoting:

'After ten years, it is shameful that Canada is not living up to the spirit and intent of the Conservation Vision and is failing to build North America's only international wildlife refuge.' Derek Coronado, Alliance coordinator, said: 'Canada needs to immediately establish a registry of lands, similar to what has been accomplished in the U.S. for the Refuge.'

We're still waiting.

*　　*　　*

ANOTHER MID-WEEK AFTERNOON. NOTHING MUCH DOING IN THE NEWSROOM.

'Where you going?'

'Out to see what's what,' I said.

'Something for tomorrow's paper, perhaps?'

'Perhaps.'

I wasn't thinking of tomorrow's paper. I was thinking of Brighton Beach. This little community I soon *wouldn't* be able to visit.

I dropped in at Bronson's, had a beer. Then went prospecting. I went up Healy, saw someone in the yard. Parked and said hello. Clovis Cote introduced himself. Said we ought to go in so I could meet Kathleen. So in we went. Pot of coffee on the counter.

The Cotes had lived at 631 Healy for 31 years. The house is single-storey, grey brick. Back in 1962 it wasn't much to look at: A two-bedroom bungalow. 'It ended right here.'

Clovis got up from his chair and crossed the kitchen and patted the wall. 'We expanded it out to here. And then we moved the front wall out.'

Kathleen: 'And dug out underneath. By hand. With a shovel. To create a basement. It wasn't much when we bought it. But we've made it a home. We've raised our family in this house.'

The family: Michelle, Celeste, Clovis Junior, and Jason.

Why Brighton Beach?

Clovis: 'It was quiet, and close to work (the salt mine). I liked the wilderness.' If you were to ask him, Clovis would describe himself—despite all these city-spent years—as a country boy. He grew up in Thedford Mines, Quebec, where his father worked in the asbestos mines until, at the age of 50, the doctor told him he'd die at 55 if he didn't find other work. So Clovis's father moved to Windsor and found work at Ford's.

Kathleen: 'His father worked in the mines and came from a dying town. And now ...'

Favourite characters?

Kathleen Cote: 'Mr. Pare, now, too bad he's dead. He'd have had stories to tell. He used to plow our field out back, with horses. Remember the day those horses sank to their bellies, Clovis?'

Clovis certainly did. 'I couldn't believe it. One minute they were walking along ahead of the plow, next minute they're down to their bellies in a sinkhole.'

Kathleen: 'Mister Pare figured it was an old well, or a septic tank. Lucky for him he got those horses out.'

Curious thing: Neither Kathleen nor Clovis can recall just how it was that Mister Pare managed that feat.

I asked them what it was like, when they first moved to Brighton Beach.

They remembered lots of walks. 'When you don't have any money, what else do you do? Take your kids out for a walk.'

It was on one of these walks that Kathleen discovered some graves. Right about where the Co-op elevators are now, down by the river-bank on the far side of the bush.

'There was two at least. One stone standing, the other on the ground. The one was for a baby. The other was for a woman. I think it said she died in childbirth. The name was Elliott.'

Clovis: 'Why sure. And Sprucewood used to be called Elliott

Street.' And Elliott Street would have taken you right down to where the graves were located. Mrs. Elliott's one-time farm.

Kathleen Cote: 'Do you know this isn't Brighton Beach?'

Clovis Cote: 'Brighton Beach is below (on the river-side of) Sandwich Street.' Clovis points at the kitchen floor. 'This is Yawkey.'

Kathleen: 'When we moved here, we had our own postal station. Yawkey.'

Clovis: 'There was Brighton, Yawkey and Ojibway.' Ojibway was on the other side of the bush, where Morton Terminal and the Co-op and DNN Galvanizing and Windsor Salt Mine are now. 'I used to hunt over there. The Ojibway Police were always around.'

The Ojibway Police?

Clovis: 'Oh yes. They had their own police and everything. It was a regular little community. The police station was on Sprucewood. It wasn't Sprucewood then. It was Elliott. The Chief of Police, what was his name? He was a big guy.'

I mention Archie Jamieson's little backyard shack, which was once upon a time an Ojibway police hut.

'Yes it was.'

Favourite things about living in Brighton Beach?

In no particular order: Orchards, peach and apple. Vineyards. Chicken coops. Pig pens. Horses in corrals. Gardens in most backyards. Neighbours working in those gardens. Neighbours, leaning on their hoes, talking over the fence with neighbours leaning on their hoes. Children everywhere. Conversations with friends and neighbours all Saturday afternoon and evening in the Westwood Tavern. Mrs. Hawchuk's store. Bootleggers (at least two, but Kathleen and Clovis think it prudent not to name names since the bootleggers' children are still around).

Clovis will say: 'Tony would deliver or you could pick up. He also used to have card games.'

Kathleen: 'In the spring, our yard was like a park. The flowers and the trees. Our kids planted some of those trees. You know how kids will. Bring something home and plant it. Anyone else would pull it out, but they planted it, so you cut the lawn around it.'

The kids planted lots of trees on this acre of ground down through the years. Kathleen did her share of planting too: Took cuttings from lilac bushes down by the river, the bushes which had been planted long ago by the people who lived in the cottages, now long gone. Those lilacs are thriving yet.

Clovis: 'There's an old tire hanging from a rope on a branch. Our kids used it. Their kids are swinging on the same branch their parents swung on when they were kids. The branch is all grown around the rope.'

Anything they wouldn't miss?

When Clovis Cote worked at the salt mine on midnights, he'd go up seven storeys in one of the mine buildings. From that vantage point he could see Zug Island in one direction and the lights of Devonshire Mall in the other.

'You could see those lights clear as anything until about three in the morning. Three in the morning was when they'd clean out the stacks. You'd just see a cloud of that stuff. And a minute later, you couldn't see Devonshire Mall at all. It was like it wasn't there.'

Between Zug Island and Devonshire Mall lies half of Windsor.

On the other hand: 'Our kids are going to miss this place,' said Kathleen. 'This is their home. When they were little they used to go over in the bush. They'd play and build forts and it was always safe.'

The Cotes were going to leave their home to their children. And they'd bought each of their children a lot adjacent to the home place.

An acre of ground, all told.

'This was supposed to be their inheritance.'

Still too early to head back to the newsroom—I'd become a disciple of Major Jack Kent—so I nosed up and down a few streets, then spotted Roger Hunt's two beached Mercury Marquis sedans in the drive of the little house at the end of Audrey Street. Roger zipping up his pants on the porch.

Apply the brakes.

By the time I've parked, Roger had zipped up and was walking down the drive. Big smile. 'One of the bonuses of living in Brighton Beach,' he said. 'Try that in Walkerville. What brings you back?'

A question.

'What do I like about living here?' said Roger. 'Apart from pissing off the porch? Well, you can have five, six cars in the yard and nobody cares. You can't do that in the city.' Roger nodded in the direction of his *junkyard*: Two Mercury sedans beached in the drive.

'I'm buildin' a Marquis.

'One, from two.' He smiles. 'Let's go inside.'

Inside, Shelley says hi. One of the things she remembers about growing up here: 'My father bought me and my sister a horse. A Quarter Horse. Sixteen hands tall.' She and her sister named the horse Shila and Shelley was still riding that horse when she was sixteen years old. 'We used to ride all over. Yawkey Bush (now Ojibway Park), over by the race track, down by the river. I remember a great big tree down there where the shore jutted out, but the tree's gone now and the shore's all washed away.'

Shelley kept that horse in a corral out back of the house where she grew up. 211 Page. She can see the house at 211 Page when she stands at the kitchen window of the house she and Roger Hunt now share at the end of Audrey. 'I still miss that house. And I'm living right here.'

Shrug and a smile.

'Favourite things?' says Roger. 'A big bombfire in the backyard. Music. Marshmallows. The works. That's what I like. You can party down here and nobody bothers you. Can't do that downtown.'

'I remember a neighbour's chicken out loose knocking on our door,' said Shelley.

Speaking of wildlife: A couple of years earlier, Roger and Shelley awoke in the middle of the night to the sound of music: Two hundred and fifty people, give or take a dozen, were in the field down by the river, the one the Rotary was thinking of as a park.

'We closed the window and put on the air conditioner.'

Roger's regretted that ever since.

By the time he had his wits about him next morning, his neighbour Howard was homeward bound on his antique bike—the one with the drug-store style carrier up front—and the carrier pretty near full of the last of the empties from the field down by the river.

'All I got was two beers cans.'

'The Bee Man used to live in a shack at the end of the street, where the brick house is now,' says Shelley. 'He'd give me bottles of pure honey for my mother.'

'I've got something you should see,' said Roger. We head outside, past the *junkyard* and stop at a little shack behind the garage.

It was sun-bleached, wind-creased, curly-shingled. Its doors unhinged. Until recently, two old men lived in the shack. Then one. It was weed-guarded now, humming with wind.

The place had a mattress for a side porch. Roger and I sprang across it and stepped inside. There were two rooms, each about eight feet by ten. We looked from wall to wall to wall to wall. The wallpaper was V'd where kids had pulled strips free.

'No electricity. No water. No bathroom. No nothin'. Used an outhouse over by the garage there.' Roger looked around. Shook his head. 'How they coulda lived here all those years beats me.

'Know what I wish? I wish someone woulda kept it, just the way it was when the old guys lived here.' Scraps of furniture and all. 'Kinda like a museum. There's history here.'

Too late, of course. Too bad.

Back in the kitchen:

What would they miss the most? 'I'll tell you what I won't miss,' said Roger. 'Dust is terrible when they don't oil the roads. The sewage lagoon's awful in the summer when the wind blows from that way. Zug Island can be pretty bad. I used to put lawn ornaments out in the summer. Zug Island turns them orange and brown. I don't bother putting them out anymore.'

'But sometimes the wind blows the other way.'

'Sometimes,' says Shelley, 'we'll take a blanket and something to drink and go down by the river and we'll lie there and look at the stacks across the river, the smoke coming out of them, and the stars.

'It's really beautiful.

'Plus, it's quiet.'

*   *   *

THE OTHER DAY I CAME ACROSS A LITTLE STORY I'D CLIPPED FROM *THE STAR*. Undated.

'Surrounded by mean-smelling sludge heaps, a moth-balled hydro plant, railroad tracks, a fouled watercourse and the soot-belching steel mills of Zug Island, Brighton Beach is a patch of earth crying out for urban renewal—either the man-made or the natural kind.'

Urban renewal.

I WENT OUT TO BRIGHTON BEACH THE SAME DAY.

Good thing I'd gone knocking when I did. No doors to knock on now. What was Brighton Beach will soon be the site of the Canadian end of a new international bridge. There isn't a house left standing. Many of the roads are blocked off with concrete barriers or mounds of dirt and there's not much to see except a couple of factories, some trees and scrub brush. And ghosts, of course. I can still hear their voices, see their faces. Though both the faces and the voices are fading.

So, a few final thoughts from these now-dispersed people, forced to leave the homes and the community and the river they loved. The people who so captured my imagination:

Denis Levesque rented his house from the Bee Man when the Bee Man moved out to Vancouver in 1991. The Bee Man did not take his bees with him. The hives were stacked, like so many Styrofoam beer coolers, down by the fence at the river-side of the property.

'He told me someone would come by and take of them. But no one's come.'

So there sat the hives.

'Maybe the bees were alive. Maybe they were dead.

'Who was going to lift the lid to see, eh?'

Danny Caza: 'If you gave the Bee Man a fish, he'd give you a jar of honey.'

Danny was one of the last to leave Brighton Beach, and like all his relatives and neighbours and friends, hated to go. 'It's one of the last spots on the river. It was a good area to grow up in. Troop though the bush. We'd be gone all day. We'd go over to the salt mine or the coal piles (beside the J. Clark Keith plant). The coal was three storeys high. Winter, we'd go down on a toboggan, the last bit flying through the air. Black? You wouldn't believe. One time I landed bad, hurt my leg. I had to crawl all the way home.'

Favourite things? 'You can turn around and piss outside and no-body's going to report you,' said Denis Levesque.

'You can still find coins down there by the river,' said Danny Caza. I betcha I could take you there right now and find all kinds of things. When we were kids we used to find Indian arrowheads. All kinds of them.'

Robert Caza: 'I found an old military button there one time. A pewter button. Kent Regiment. 24th Battalion.'

Danny Caza: 'Every time I go down there by the river I find something.'

Things which will not be missed? Ivy Jamieson had to think a second: 'When we moved here (1957), that's when my allergies started. I don't know what it was. At first I thought it was a summer cold. I don't know what we're breathing. But black dust seeps through the windows. And we've got double windows. It's certainly not clean air.'

What Denis Levesque particularly liked about the Bee Man's house, as soon as he spotted it, was the garden (about an acre) and the rest of the grounds (another two), and the fence all around the property, a fence interwoven with vines.

'I've got 12 peach trees and 12 pear trees plus the garden.

'If you want to be in touch with Mother Nature you've got to get your hands in the dirt. Some people, they like to sit in front of the TV or in the hotel. Me? I like my garden.'

He'd always liked gardening, ever since he was a kid back in New Brunswick. He'd have been in his thirties when I spoke with him. Still spent his spare time in that garden.

Something else he loved: A view of the river between all the trees in the field. Zug Island as well, of course. But mainly the river. And he loved the space. There was a woodlot behind the house, a vacant field between the house and the river and fields between his place and the nearest neighbours, whose names he does not know.

'I like the people out here all right. But when it comes to living my own private life, I want to be by myself.

'Here, you got solitude. If you want to be at peace with yourself, you need to be apart.'

'Out here, nobody bothers me.'

Until a few weeks before I met him, the field beside his rented house was all green, lots of trees, a kind of meadow that someone had forgotten about. Then someone remembered it.

Bulldozers and earth scrapers lumbered in. By the time I knocked on Denis' door, most of the topsoil has been scraped up and trucked away. The trees had been bulldozed. No one in the neighbourhood seemed to know why, or by whom. Well, they knew the 'why' part. It's what happens when a city decides to hand over a big patch of prime land to industry.

Denis Levesque: 'There's so much green land being destroyed. You'll never get it back. What about our children? We have to leave them something.'

Denis looked at the denuded field, then at the fuming mills of Zug Island, and then excused himself. He had to get back to work on his Grand Am. A brake line let go.

I wished him luck.

'Shouldn't be a problem.'

He was talking about the brake line.

*　　　*　　　*

SO THESE WERE MY RIVER PEOPLE. THEY EXPERIENCED THE RIVER AS FEW others in Windsor do. They swam in the river, fished in the river, drank by the river, made music by the river, made love by the river, slept by the river under a ceiling of stars. The river was rarely out of sight, never out of their thoughts. It defined who they were.

What remains with me from all my wanderings door to door, half an hour here, an hour there, coffee in this kitchen, beer in that living room, chatting with the people who lived in Brighton Beach, was their overarching love of this little place they called home down by the river on the sorry side of town. Melancholy. And a mystery, I'm sure, to anyone who simply drove through to have a beer at The Westwood or dump some of their junk at the end of a lane.

When you sit in an outhouse with the door open looking at the stars above the plumes of Zug Island like Doug Todd once did, when you hear a freighter thrumming past, when you *feel* the freighter—its vibrations coming through the water, up through the earth, and up through the wooden boards—you *feel* the river the way few other people possible can: In your bones.

In a way, whether we live right beside the river or not, the river defines the rest of us as well. We are, all of us, river people.

* * *

IF I HAVE TO EAT CROW, I GENERALLY LIKE IT MEDIUM RARE, HOLD THE feathers. I waited what seemed an appropriate face-saving amount of time. A month, as I recall.

'Hi,' I said. 'It's the asshole.'

'I was hoping you'd call. Let me check my calendar.' He put me on hold. Came back on the line. 'How about tomorrow afternoon? Say one o'clock.' I was tempted to say 'Let me check my calendar,' but he'd had enough of me being an asshole already. 'Right. Good.'

'You know where to find me?'

He gave me directions. And the following afternoon, five to one, there I was, standing in his office. He checked his watch. 'Prompt,' he said.

'It's what happens when you get fired one time for being late.'

'Tell me more,' he said.

So I told him. This was back in my Owen Sound days. Art Davidson had hired me as a reporter, but then thought I should get a little experience on the wire desk. Start time 4 AM. Pretty cool job. You got to rip all the stories off the teletype machine—they came in on a big roll of paper—and separate the stories and then decide which ones you should put on which page. Heavy duty.

So I set two alarms and slept through them both, woke up at around six in a cold sweat, drove like a maniac down to *The Sun-Times*, came to a screeching halt, ran up the stairs. Art, all alone at the wire desk, looked at me: 'You're no use to me now.'

So, now what?

'Go home,' he said.

'Home?'

'You're fired.'

Rod laughed.

'What I didn't know was that as soon as I left, Art phoned my mother, told her what he'd done. Told her not to let me get another job.

He'd give me a call in a week or so. It would be a good lesson, he said.'

'Seems to have sunk in,' said Rod.

'Now and then lessons do.'

'Ever been on campus before?'

I shook my head.

'Why don't we take a tour?'

Fine. I was up for that. Seemed harmless.

Rod wanted to know if I'd ever thought of going to university. I laughed. I told him school and I hadn't gotten along all that well. 'I failed Grade 9, then passed Grade 9 and Grade 10, and failed Grade 11 and then passed Grade 11 and squeaked out of Grade 12 with a 52% average. Actually, I probably failed Grade 12, but they were so sick of me, they passed me just to get rid of me.'

'Being an asshole?'

'Yeah. But I wasn't the only one. A few of the teachers qualified.'

'No doubt,' said Rod. He was smiling as he said so. 'This is Memorial Hall,' he said. We went in through the big wooden doors, looked at some classrooms. 'This is where most of the first-year classes are.' We went out another door to the library. Then we went back to the building where his office was, up some stairs, down a corridor. 'This is the philosophy department,' said Rod. He introduced me to the head of the department, and then to a couple of the professors we passed in the hall. 'Paul Vasey. From *The Star*. You've been reading his stories in the paper.'

Then we went to the English Department and the History Department, the Geography Department. Same thing. 'I'd like you to meet the head of the department ...' Saying hi and shaking hands everywhere we went. Then we went back to his office.

'You're all set,' he said.

'All set?' I said.

'You start in September.'

'Start? September?'

'What do you think we were just doing? You're enrolled. Ready to go. Now all you have to do is decide.'

'Whether or not I want to go on being an asshole?'

'Something like that,' he said. Curious smile.

'I'll have to think this through.'

'Now there's a good first step,' he said. He shook my hand. 'Give me a call.'

'I will.'

'Tomorrow,' he said.

Tomorrow?

I went down the elevator and out the door and back the way we'd just come. Took a look at Memorial Hall and the other buildings. I remember thinking, 'Wow.' Nobody in my family had ever been to university. How cool was this? I spent half an hour or so just wandering around campus, nosing through the bookstore. I don't think life had ever felt as full of possibilities as it did just then.

I could have gone right back up to Rod's office. But I waited. Called him the next day.

And the rest, as they say …

I had a little chat with Norm Hull. Told him I'd like to switch from reporting to working the overnight editing desk. That way I could go to university during the day and work at night.

'You're sure you can do that?'

'No, but I'll give it a try.'

'You do that.'

And I did that and three years later, look what I was holding rolled up in my left hand as I crossed the stage and shook hands with J. Francis Leddy. 'Congratulations,' said the president of the university.

Next hand I shook was Rod Scott's.

'Thanks,' I said.

'Don't mention it,' he said.

'Can I buy you a drink?'

'Always.'

Time is a fast old train
So sang Townes Van Zandt.
She's here and she's gone
and she won't come again

I'VE BEEN THINKING A LOT ABOUT TIME LATELY, TIME AND THE NATURE OF fate. How that fast old train, for no apparent reason—given the infinite possibilities—takes us down one track rather than another. How things change as a result of that in ways we'll never know. How one thing tends to lead surprisingly to another. That call Art Davidson made all those years ago, which led to the call from the girl I'd become chums with, asking me to come stay with her and her friend, which led to a wedding ceremony, which led to that strange encounter with Rod Scott one night in The Press Club, which led to .... You get a serious case of the *what ifs*. I sometimes wonder—it will drive you crazy if you think about it for too long—how life would have turned out if only *one* of those had never happened.

If I had never quit my job at *The Owen Sound Sun-Times* to become a salesman, and if I'd never quit that salesman's job and gone back to see Art Davidson, would I ever have found my way to Windsor? Would I ever have worked at *The Windsor Star*, married the woman I did, had the children and grandchildren we have, met all these people who loom so large in my memory and imagination? You'd have to say, no, none of those things would have happened. My life would have turned out completely differently. But just how, I'll never know. And that's fine.

I'd say the fates have conspired to place me where I was at the moment I should have been there, encountering the people I needed to know, nudging me this way and that along the road of the life I've lived from way back then to right this moment. I'm sitting under the awning on our back patio on a sunny summer Thursday afternoon, listening to the birds at their feeders. Through the open windows behind me, I can hear the brown-eyed girl stirring inside the house, as I am writing all of this down.

Many years ago I was walking with my pal Kevin Doyle from *The Star* to Lee's, and we passed a sewer grate—an ungodly stink. We reeled away from it and Kevin said—I think he shouted, actually—'I don't want to die in this fucking town!' The sewer gas seemed a perfect metaphor for what was ahead of us if we didn't get out of Windsor soon, and for good.

None of us saw Windsor as a place we'd wind up in. We were afflicted with overweening ambition. We had to be—*had to be*—destined for grander things: *The Globe and Mail, The New York Times, The Guardian*. At the very least. Hubris was not wanting.

Worked for Kevin. He went on to become editor of *Maclean's Magazine*. I left as well, did a stint at *The Canadian Press* in Toronto, then joined *The Spectator* in Hamilton, and was settling in as a kind of self-appointed (lots of front-page bylines) prima donna. Seemed like we were in for the long haul, we were even looking for a house down around the university. And then …

April 3, 1974: A tornado brought down the Windsor Curling Club and my brown-eyed girl's dad, Nick Haddad, was one of the nine killed.

You can't imagine.

I'd never written a eulogy. There's a first time for everything:

Nick Haddad walked among men in a special way. He walked straight but not unbending. He walked proudly but not arrogantly. He walked hastily but not past those who needed him. He filled a very great space. He filled that space with laughter. He filled that space with smiles. He filled that space with understanding. He filled that space with kindness. And now he leaves a very great void. But he does not leave us empty.

He came into our lives and will not leave. A part of him remains. Someone told me once that where there are memories there is no death. Such memories we have, all of us. For my part, the memories are happy.

I see him in his store working hard but taking time for a quick joke. I see him at his curling club frowning at a bad rock, laughing in the lounge. I see him most of all in our home for that is where he truly lived. With his family whom he loved as he loved life itself.

I see him fast asleep before the television, snoring. I see him playing cards at the kitchen table. I see him in his swimming pool, happy because his family or his friends are with him. I see him in a hundred ways. I will always see Nick Haddad.

He was a kind and decent man. He was hard-working and honest. He was warm and open. He was not a simply man but he was a man of simple tastes. He cared not for the excesses which wealth affords, nor the fleeting illusions which are power and fame.

He was a man who truly understood where he had been and where he was going. He was a man, it seemed to me, who was at peace with himself. I am proud to have known him and to have been loved by him.

YOU LOSE SOMEONE THAT WAY, SO SUDDENLY, SO HORRIFICALLY, YOU FEEL the whole earth lurching and shifting beneath your feet, and all you want to do is get back on any solid ground you can find. All we wanted to do was come back home, however different home would be from then on. So a couple of days after the funeral I went down to *The Star*, asked if I could come back.

Who knows how our lives would have turned out if none of this happened, if we'd gone back to Hamilton, bought that house. The one thing I do know: I'd never have received a call one day years later and out of the blue from the manager of the local CBC Radio station. They were looking for a morning-show host and they wanted a newsman, not an announcer, to do the job. 'Are you crazy?' I said. 'I've never done radio.' 'We can teach you radio,' he said. 'It's the newsman I'm after.' A decade-and-a-half later, another call out of the blue: Would I consider taking the morning show in Victoria?

So we got all the way to Vancouver Island. Now, if anything was going to finally wrest us from *Winzer,* you'd think that would do the trick—all those mountains, all that ocean, all those old-growth forests. And look at me now. Right back home. *Home.* And couldn't wait to get back. The place had a grip on me, something I'd never have imagined all those years ago when Kevin and I vowed we would make the great escape.

My pal Dan Wells says that when he was a kid, his family would drive to Windsor from Chatham, and his overriding sense of the place was that it was grey. *All grey.* A dingy, dreary little border town. It's only now, after many years living here, that he's begun to detect a little colour in its cheeks. The colour was there all along. Just took some time to see it. Works on you that way, this old river town. Worked on me.

There's still a chance you'll be overwhelmed, as Kevin and I were, as you walk past a sewer grate. But there are sewer grates everywhere. Which didn't occur to Kevin and me at the time. I've lived here longer now than I've lived any place else. And I've come to see that it's exactly the place I should be. Fits me, this town. Fits me just fine.

Ask anyone what they love most about *Winzer,* what gives the place its colour, and they seem always to tell you it's the people, the family and friends, neighbours and acquaintances webbed around each of us. True. But for me the town is also, and perhaps mainly, the larger-than-life characters who ghost around in my imagination and my memory: rumrunners and prize fighters and elegant old ladies and one-eyed thugs and earnest well-meaning politicians and hucksters and hookers and crusty old editors.

Many of them I remember meeting.

Some of them I actually met.

You've heard it said that 'If he didn't exist, I'd have to invent him'? Yes, well.

So, she said. Did these things really happen?

Oh yes, he said.

All of them?

I'd say so. Most of them, anyway.

Most of them?

To the best of my recollection, he said.

And the people? she said. Did they exist?

Oh yes, he said.

All of them?

All of them.

One way, or another.

Which is memory, which is dream? And does it matter—
aren't they finally both the same?
                    —Graeme Gibson, *Gentleman Death*

ACKNOWLEDGEMENTS

Thanks to

    .... my faithful early versions reading crew: Marilyn, Kirsten and Adam and Jacquie and Phil Gibson.

    .... my always helpful friends at the downtown branch of The Windsor Public Library.

    ... Mary Popovich for her careful copy-edit of the manuscript and her many suggestions for improving it.

    ... and, especially, Dan Wells, without whose encouragement and enthusiasm (and gentle pestering) this book would never have seen the light of day.

PAUL VASEY is the author of about a dozen books—non-fiction, short stories and novels—including the critically acclaimed *A Troublesome Boy,* published last year by Groundwood Books/House of Anansi in Toronto. For 18 years he hosted the CBC Radio morning show in Windsor and in Victoria, B.C. Prior to joining the CBC, Vasey was an award-winning reporter and feature writer with several newspapers, including *The Windsor Star.* He graduated from The University of Windsor with a Bachelor of Arts degree in philosophy and later spent a year at Massey College in the University of Toronto while on a Southam Fellowship. This would have come as stunning news to the teachers who failed him in Grade 9 and Grade 11. He and his wife Marilyn live in Windsor. They have two children and four grandchildren.